MEL BOU RNE NOW

CO-AAV-629

Exhibition Guide

ngv
National
Gallery of
Victoria

This publication has been generously
supported by the Vizard Foundation.

CONTENTS

FOREWORD

Melbourne Now is an exhibition unlike any other we have mounted at the National Gallery of Victoria. It takes as its premise the idea that a city is significantly shaped by the artists, designers, architects, choreographers, intellectuals and community groups that live and work in its midst. With this in mind, we have set out to explore how Melbourne's visual artists and creative practitioners contribute to the dynamic cultural identity of this city. The result is an exhibition that celebrates what is unique about Melbourne's art, design and architecture communities.

When we began the process of creating *Melbourne Now* we envisaged using several gallery spaces within The Ian Potter Centre: NGV Australia; soon, however, we recognised that the number of outstanding Melbourne practitioners required us to greatly expand our commitment. Now spreading over both The Ian Potter Centre: NGV Australia and NGV International, *Melbourne Now* encompasses more than 8000 square metres of exhibition space, making it the largest single show ever presented by the Gallery.

Melbourne Now represents a new way of working for the NGV. We have adopted a collaborative curatorial approach which has seen twenty of our curators work closely with both external design curators and many other members of the NGV team. Committing to this degree of research and development has provided a great opportunity to meet with artists in their studios and to engage with colleagues across the city as a platform not only for this exhibition, but also for long-term engagement.

A primary aim throughout the planning process has been to create an exhibition that offers dynamic engagement with our audiences. From the minute visitors enter NGV International they are invited to participate through the exhibition's *Community Hall* project, which offers a diverse program of performances, talks, presentations and events that showcase a broad concept of creativity across all art forms, including choirs, dance performances, music, fashion parades and show-and-tells. Entering the galleries, visitors discover that *Melbourne Now* includes ambitious and exciting contemporary art and design commissions in a wide range of media by emerging and established artists. We are especially proud of the design and architectural components of this exhibition which, for the first time, place these important areas of practice in the context of a wider survey of contemporary art. We have designed the exhibition in terms of a series of curated, interconnected installations and 'exhibitions within the exhibition' to offer an immersive, inclusive and sometimes participatory experience.

Viewers will find many new art commissions featured as keynote projects of *Melbourne Now*. One special element is a series of commissions developed specifically for children and young audiences – these works encourage participatory learning for kids and families. Artistic commissions extend from the visual arts to architecture, dance and choreography to reflect Melbourne's diverse artistic expression. Many of the new visual arts and design commissions will be acquired for the Gallery's permanent collections, leaving the people of Victoria a lasting legacy of *Melbourne Now*.

The intention of this exhibition is to encourage and inspire everyone to discover some of the best of Melbourne's culture. To help achieve this, family-friendly activities, dance and music performances, inspiring talks from creative practitioners, city walks and ephemeral installations and events make up our public programs. Whatever your creative interests, there will be a lot to learn and enjoy in *Melbourne Now*.

Melbourne Now is a major project for the NGV which we hope will have a profound and lasting impact on our audiences, our engagement with the art communities in our city and on the NGV collection. We invite you to join us in enjoying some of the best of Melbourne's creative art, design and architecture in this landmark exhibition.

Tony Ellwood
Director, National Gallery of Victoria

Acknowledgements

The NGV is thrilled that this exhibition has struck a chord with Melbourne's passionate philanthropic community and seen a commitment from government and the corporate sector. Thank you to the Victorian Government for the outstanding support of *Melbourne Now* and our summer season initiative. In particular, I would like to thank The Honourable Denis Napthine MP, Premier of Victoria, and The Honourable Heidi Victoria MP, Minister for the Arts, for their great leadership in backing these new seasonal and curatorial approaches.

The corporate community has also demonstrated great leadership by getting behind *Melbourne Now* and its programs, and I gratefully thank our Principal Partner Mercedes-Benz Australia/Pacific and Horst von Sanden; Major Partners Ernst & Young and Gerard Dalbosco, Bank of Melbourne and Scott Tanner, the City of Melbourne and the Lord Mayor Robert Doyle, and Higgins Coatings and John Higgins; and Learning Partner La Trobe University and Vice-Chancellor, Professor John Dewar. We are extremely thankful for the support of our Media and Tourism Sponsors The Herald & Weekly Times and Peter Clark, 774 ABC Melbourne and Randal Mathieson and Cath Hurley, the Seven Network and Tim Worner, DMG Radio and Cathy O'Connor, Val Morgan and Damian Keogh AM, APN Outdoor and Richard Herring, Adshel and Rob Atkinson, V/Line and Theo Taifalos, Melbourne Airport and Chris Woodruff, Sofitel Melbourne On Collins and Clive Scott, and Clemenger BBDO and Peter Biggs. I thank our Support Sponsors Egon Zehnder International and Christopher Thomas, Dulux Australia and Patrick Houlihan, and Mecca Cosmetica and Joanna Horgan. I also wish to thank the Australia Council for the Arts and Tony Grybowski, as well as VicHealth and Jerril Rechter for their vital contributions to *Melbourne Now*.

Many individuals have assisted this exhibition with substantial private support, including our *Melbourne Now* Champions the Dewhurst family and Robin Campbell and Bruce Parncutt, whose support has enabled the delivery of an extensive program for children and the introduction of new technology to underpin the visitors' experience. I would like to thank the Spotlight Charitable Foundation, whose support has made the transformation of our sculpture garden possible, Harold and Krystyna Campbell-Pretty, who are funding a program that will enable school children from across Victoria to access *Melbourne Now*, and Professor Andrew Vizard of the Vizard Foundation, who has backed the creation of the *Melbourne Now* limited-edition publication, exhibition guide and ebook. In addition, I would like to thank the Truby and Florence Williams Charitable Trust, The Hugh D. T. Williamson Foundation, the Bowness Family Foundation, the Michael and Andrew Buxton Foundation, Michael and Janet Buxton, Joan Clemenger and Peter Clemenger AM, Peter and Monica Edwards, Esther and David Frenkiel, Kerry Gardner and Andrew Myer, Alistair Hay, Julie, Michael and Silvia Kantor, Corbett and Yueji Lyon, The John McCaughey Memorial Prize Trust, Fiona and Sidney Myer AM, the Myer Foundation, the NGV Foundation 2013 Annual Dinner Donors, NGV Supporters of Contemporary Art, The Orloff Family Charitable Trust, Loris Orthwein, The Ian Potter Foundation, the Agnes Robertson Fund, a sub-fund of the Australian Communities Foundation, the Robert Salzer Foundation, the Loti and Victor Smorgon Fund, The Sunraysia Foundation, Wai Tang and Kee Wong, Tam Vu, Vitae Partners, and the Yulgilbar Foundation, whose support has assisted the creation of numerous artistic commissions that make *Melbourne Now* an unforgettable experience.

I would also like to take this opportunity to thank our Council of Trustees President Bruce Parncutt, Professor Su Baker, Dr Susan Cohn, The Honourable Linda Dessau AM, Peter Edwards, Corbett Lyon, Vicki Pearce, Andrew Sisson, Michael Ullmer and Jason Yeap OAM for their commitment and resolute belief in what we hope to achieve through *Melbourne Now*. Finally, I wish to thank my Executive Management Team, Andrew Clark and Dr Isobel Crombie, and the dedicated NGV staff whose hard work, creativity and determination has brought this ambitious exhibition to life. Every department has made a meaningful contribution to *Melbourne Now*, and its success is due to their unwavering enthusiasm for pushing the boundaries of what we can achieve.

Tony Ellwood
Director, National Gallery of Victoria

SPONSOR'S MESSAGE

At Mercedes-Benz, fascination and art are part of our DNA. Contemporary design and distinctive style are key pillars of our brand. From creative and innovative expression flourish great ideas. After seven consecutive years as Principal Partner of major exhibitions at the National Gallery of Victoria, Mercedes-Benz is thrilled to support the NGV in its new collaborative approach to working with artists, curators and audiences for *Melbourne Now*.

Melbourne is one of the world's truly great cities. We take great pride in playing but a small role in bringing to life *Melbourne Now*, a celebration of the art, design and architecture that shapes this city.

Encompassing a wide range of works, *Melbourne Now* represents a new direction for the NGV and includes something for everyone – from emerging and established artists' projects and commissions for children and families, to architecture and design initiatives and curatorial engagement with dance, performance, music and sound.

We trust you and your family will delight in *Melbourne Now*.

Horst von Sanden,
Managing Director,
Mercedes-Benz Cars

 Mercedes-Benz

Presented by

Principal Partner

Major Partners

Melbourne Now Champions

Dewhurst family
Robin Campbell and Bruce Parncutt

Melbourne Now Major Donor

Spotlight Charitable Foundation

Partner

Learning Partner

  This project has been assisted
by the Australian Government
through the Australia Council,
its arts funding and advisory body

Media and Tourism Sponsors

Herald Sun

 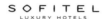 

Government and Foundation Supporters

Support Sponsors

MAPS

LEGEND

NGVA   The Ian Potter Centre: NGV Australia
NGVI   NGV International

F   Foyer
FC   Federation Court
GEG   Grollo Equiset Garden
GH   Great Hall
SA   Studio A
SB   Studio B
SC   Studio C

OFF SITE AND OTHER LOCATIONS

ALLYOURWALLS – Hosier Lane, Melbourne

On Top of the World: Flags for Melbourne –
16 sites across the city of Melbourne

Wired for Melbourne Sound – EP by Batman Park
played in ambient spaces at The Ian Potter
Centre: NGV Australia and NGV International

NGV International, Ground Floor

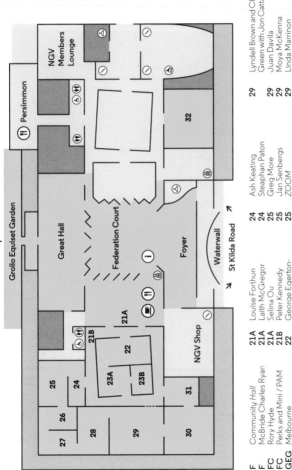

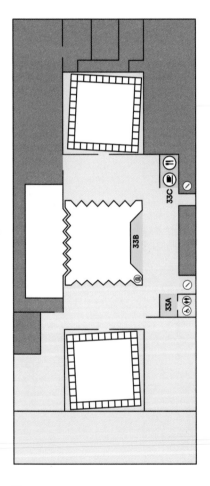

33A *The Donkey's Tail Jnr*
33B Alan Constable
33C Kristin McIver
33C *Melbourne Design Now*

NGV International, Level 3

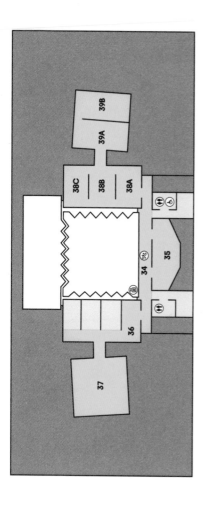

NGV Australia, Ground Floor

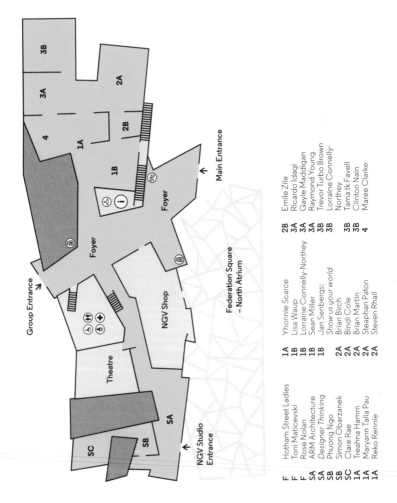

NGV Australia, Level 2

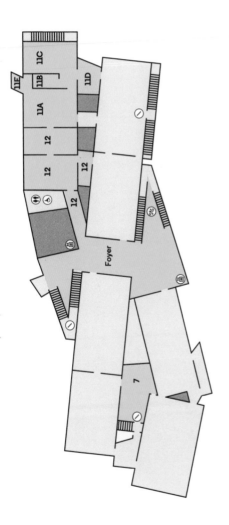

NGV Australia, Level 3

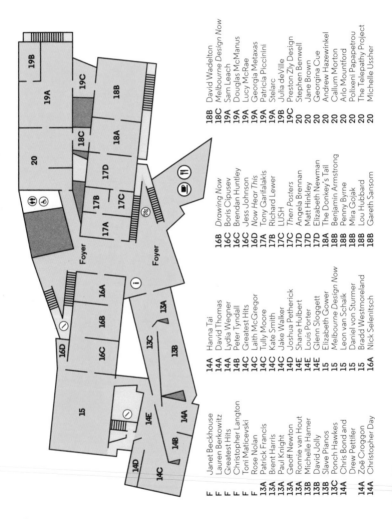

THE ARTISTS

A CONSTRUCTED WORLD

NGVI, Level 3, Gallery 37

A Constructed World is the moniker of the influential artistic collaboration between Geoff Lowe and Jacqueline Riva. Active since 1993, and currently based in Paris, A Constructed World's projects encompass painting and video, publishing and performance, workshops and events. Often involving improvisation, free association and the choreography of multiple participants and perspectives, Lowe and Riva's practice encourages risk, response and unexpected encounters in an investigation of the act of making art.

For *Melbourne Now*, A Constructed World reflects on the shift towards neoliberalism and economic rationalism that has occurred over the past decade, during which Lowe and Riva have mostly lived abroad. Informed by a period of research undertaken with French philosopher Fabien Vallos and the artists' extended collaborative group Speech and What Archive, A Constructed World explores Aristotle's notion of the Chrematistic: the process of accumulating wealth through money and goods regardless of their use value. The resulting combination of works – one painting, one video and one sculpture – references the parable of the talents from Matthew 25: 14–30 and explores the embarrassment and conscious duplicity of this story and its implications. JW

A Constructed World
The parable of the talents
2013 (still)

ALLYOURWALLS

Hosier Lane, Melbourne

Located in central Melbourne (between Flinders Lane and Flinders Street and running parallel to Russell Street), Hosier Lane, along with its cobbled 'anabranch' Rutledge Lane, first came to prominence as a venue for street art in the 1990s. Since then, the walls of the lanes have functioned as an exhibition site for local and visiting international street artists. Recently, several organisations have been working with local artists to invigorate Hosier Lane with a diverse range of projects. Among the organisations fostering dynamic art events within Hosier Lane are notable Melbourne street art blog *Land of Sunshine*, *Invurt* – one of Australia's leading online underground art magazines – and Hosier Inc, a community association comprising residents, property owners and artists.

ALLYOURWALLS has been organised by *Land of Sunshine* and *Invurt* in association with the National Gallery of Victoria and Hosier Inc, and forms a key component of *Melbourne Now*. It brings together some of Melbourne's finest street artists and graffiti crews in a major makeover of Hosier Lane that celebrates the significant role street art and graffiti continues to play in the cultural life of this city. **DH**

Hosier Lane looking towards
Federation Square 2013

RICK AMOR

NGVI, Ground Floor, Gallery 23A

Rick Amor has been involved in artmaking, more specifically painting, sculpture and printmaking, for the past forty-five years. Amor's world is a rich composition of his life aesthetic and experiences played out through his work. He has held more than fifty solo shows and is represented in major public and private collections in Australia and internationally.

Best known for his brooding urban landscapes, Amor's work in *Melbourne Now*, *Mobile call*, 2012, stays true to this theme. The painting speaks to the heart of urban living in its depiction of a darkened city alleyway, with dim, foreboding lighting. A security camera on the wall surveys the scene, a lone, austere figure just within its watch. The camera represents the omnipresent surveillance of our modern lives, and an uneasy air of suspicion permeates the painting's subdued, grey landscape. Amor's reflections on the urban landscape are solemn, restrained and often melancholic. Quietly powerful, his work alludes to a mystery in the banality of daily existence. *Mobile call* is a realistic portrayal of a metropolitan landscape that opens our eyes to a strange and complex world. **MP**

Rick Amor
Mobile call 2012
Private collection, Melbourne

ARM ARCHITECTURE

NGVA, Ground Floor, Studio A

ARM Architecture was founded in 1988 by Stephen Ashton, Howard Raggatt and Ian McDougall, and is one of Australia's most inventive and polemical architectural practices. Their work is characterised by formally complex and intellectually rich buildings which inspire both praise and venom. Buildings by ARM include RMIT University's Storey Hall (1992–96), National Museum of Australia (1997–2001), Melbourne Shrine of Remembrance Visitor Centre (2000–03, 2012–), Marion Cultural Centre (1999–2001), Melbourne Theatre Company's Southbank Theatre (2002–08), Melbourne Recital Centre (2002–08), and the redevelopment of Hamer Hall (2009–12).

For *Melbourne Now*, ARM will set up office in The Ian Potter Centre: NGV Australia, establishing NGV Studio as an incubator for urban research. Occupying the gallery with a rotating contingent of architects, colleagues and guests, ARM will act as a curator of activities and events, and catalyst for new research and propositions related to critical sites in and around Melbourne. MD

ARM Architecture
*Hamer Hall redevelopment,
Southbank* 2009–12

BENJAMIN ARMSTRONG

Prolific multidisciplinary artist Benjamin Armstrong was born in Melbourne in 1975. He graduated from the Victorian College of the Arts with a Bachelor of Fine Art in 1996 and since then has widely exhibited his work, ranging from sculpture to works on paper, in Australia and abroad. Armstrong's distinctive style is intriguing, adventurous and also slightly unsettling: his experimentation and play with visceral, sensual forms, patterns and materials provokes strong reactions in the viewer.

The large-scale works on paper by Armstrong included in *Melbourne Now* are no different. These pieces are charged with a mysterious energy that is pregnant with potential, signifying transformation, turbulence and instability. Each work carries loose, swirling watercolour forms which suggest hovering emotional and physical forces to be contended with. The charged and powerful tentacles in *Conjuring*, 2011, reveal a vastly different tone to that of *Victory*, 2011, where beams of light crack through a looming, dark sky, eliciting slight optimism. Individually and collectively these works pose big questions about our world, our geographies and our origins. **NA**

Benjamin Armstrong
Conjuring 2011

JANET BECKHOUSE

Janet Beckhouse is one of Melbourne's foremost contemporary ceramicists. Her sculptural forms are influenced by the aesthetics of Baroque and Rococo ornamentation, fifteenth-century majolica ware and early twentieth-century Australian ceramic traditions. Beckhouse completed a Bachelor of Fine Art at RMIT University in 2000, and a Master of Fine Art at Monash University in 2012. She has exhibited widely in Australia during the past decade.

Beckhouse's elaborate creations often have a melancholic air and impart a sense of dark folklore. Skulls and bones – symbols of the fragility of human existence and the inevitability of our mortality – are recurring motifs and lend her oeuvre a contemporary streetwise currency. References to the natural world, from lizards, snakes and sea creatures to intricate plants and elaborate corals, also punctuate her work. Characterised by a visual cacophony of forms and references, Beckhouse's art is one of contrasts. As fellow ceramicist Peter Pilven observed, 'Like the music of Jimi Hendrix, whom she admires, [Beckhouse's] creations often convey a discordant spikiness that can contrast and clash, creating a visual disharmony that is not always pretty or comfortable.' JW

Janet Beckhouse
Portsea 2013

STEPHEN BENWELL

Stephen Benwell's practice, which has spanned a period of almost forty years, includes print-making, drawing and painting; however, he is best known for his distinctive hand-built and freely decorated ceramic forms and figures. Benwell began his professional career in 1975 and since then has held more than thirty solo exhibitions – most recently a major survey exhibition in 2013 at Heide Museum of Modern Art, Melbourne. His work typically integrates elements of classical history with a lyrical artistic aesthetic and unconventional approach to the ceramic medium.

Throughout his career a major preoccupation of Benwell's work has been the depiction of the male figure. In 2006 he commenced a series of figurative sculptural works that explore issues relating to masculinity, naked beauty and sensuality. These works, initially inspired by eighteenth-century figurines and Greco-Roman statuary, have become a significant aspect of Benwell's recent practice. The artist contributes a group of these evocative male figures for *Melbourne Now*. DH

Stephen Benwell
Statue, arm raised 2011

LAUREN BERKOWITZ

Nature and the environment are constant themes of Lauren Berkowitz's artistic practice. Her works reflect on the role of nature in biblical narratives and ancient myths – stories which address the importance placed on landscape by the people who utilise it. Inspired by the natural world, but troubled by its degradation, Berkowitz recycles materials to create environmental narratives in an act of regeneration. Her post-Minimalist sculptures are a hybrid form of temporal, process-based installation.

Berkowitz's installation for *Melbourne Now* is a sensory indoor garden which utilises edible and medicinal plants that have healing qualities in traditional and Western medicines. While referencing the Chelsea Physic Garden, London, and the Victory gardens of the First and Second World Wars, this living artwork embodies notions of renewal and sustainability, with the plants cultivated in recycled plastic pots, bottles and takeaway containers. *Physic garden*, 2013, creates an aromatic and immersive experience for the viewer, inviting reflection on the Australian landscape and its transformations throughout history. JW

Lauren Berkowitz
Manna 2009

The commission for *Melbourne Now* is supported by Peter and Monica Edwards

BRIAN BIRCH

Brian Birch was born in Fitzroy in 1936, where he grew up in straitened circumstances with his mother and grandmother, who were of Wurundjeri descent. Birch was unaware of his Aboriginality until he was thirty-seven, when he was first told about his family history by Koori elder Bobby Lovett. In 2006 Birch attended Koori art classes at NMIT, Preston, in which he came to painting intuitively and swiftly developed his own vocabulary.

Inspired by the colour and spontaneous style of Vincent van Gogh, Birch paints with freedom of expression and vibrant brushstrokes and has conceived an iconography of meanders, circles and gestural markings to express his spiritual identity. *Koori elders dancing*, 2012, invokes the power of spirited dancing in celebration of male elders giving away their daughters in marriage. The work causes Birch to honour the beauty and mourn the loss of his wife, Laraine, and his mother, Rose. The large roundels, emblematic of two *Ngurungaeta* (headmen), surrounded by lines of small and large circles – which cannot be broken – echo the tiered compositions of William Barak's corroboree drawings. JR

Brian Birch
Koori elders dancing 2012

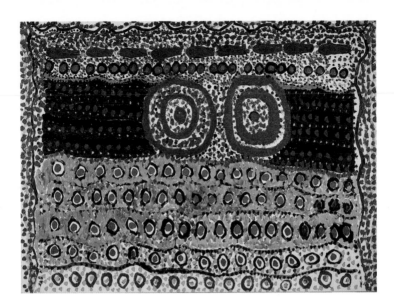

CHRIS BOND AND DREW PETTIFER

NGVA, Level 3, Gallery 14A

Chris Bond studied fine art at RMIT University, Melbourne. He makes work that charts the decline and fall of artistic idealism. Bond creates parallel worlds of seeming authenticity by constructing fictitious identities, transforming found objects into painted artefacts, simulating standard modes of artistic presentation and rewriting art history. Drew Pettifer studied law, arts and arts management at the University of Melbourne and RMIT University and is currently undertaking a doctorate in photomedia at Monash University. Pettifer's practice explores themes of intimacy, gender, sexuality and the politics of the gaze using photography, video, installation and performance. His subjects are usually young men through whom he explores the private and public act of desire.

For *Melbourne Now*, Bond and Pettifer have worked collaboratively to create diptychs, initiating a dialogue between their respective photography and painting practices. Pettifer exhibits photographs of young men, while in accompanying duplicate images Bond paints over the figures so as to make them disappear. The presence and absence of the human subjects instils these works with a strong sense of loss and longing. RL

Drew Pettifer
Untitled (Benjamin in a tree) 2011

Chris Bond
Drew Pettifer
Untitled (Benjamin in a tree, erased) 2011

Supported by the Bowness Family Foundation

STEPHEN BRAM

For more than two decades, Stephen Bram has developed a body of work exploring the relationship between abstract painting and the representation of architectural space. His easel and mural-scale wall paintings, installations and architecture, and film and light installations are determined according to very specific rules: the designation of two, sometimes three, perspectival points in space as coordinates that inform the works' shapes, and to which each work refers.

Bram's *Level 3, E29, NGV*, 2013, is an architectural installation constructed according to designated vanishing points beyond the frame of the National Gallery of Victoria's architecture. Built from conventional materials – steel, wood, plasterboard and paint – it is both an object (sculpture) and an enclosed space (architecture). The work's dynamic planes subject the viewer to new perspectives and perceptions of space. Bram's work is formalist and self-referential, but at the same time refers to the real world renounced by purely formalist painting and sculpture. As an autonomous structure, it is nevertheless continuous with the world outside, and exceeds its objective limits by pointing to the existence of a world beyond. **MD**

Stephen Bram
Untitled 2009
installation view, Ian Potter
Museum of Art, University
of Melbourne

The commission for
Melbourne Now is supported
by the Michael and Andrew
Buxton Foundation

ANGELA BRENNAN

For more than two decades, Angela Brennan has been well regarded as a painter of highly coloured abstract shapes, playful texts, and laconic philosophical musings. At once cerebral and tactile, her work is marked by an irreverent humour and introduces a ribald, libidinous and sometimes lawless subjectivity into the formal realm of modernist painting. More recently, Brennan has returned to a childhood passion of making ceramics.

For *Melbourne Now*, Brennan presents a trove of funky, wonky vessels, orbs and figures. Sometimes hand-built, other times thrown on the wheel, these works lovingly reference Bronze and Iron Age artefacts, ceramics of Anatolian and Cypriot provenance the artist encountered on travels and in local museum collections, as well as antiquities and *objets trouvés* collected over the years. With an amateur yet studied technical experimentation, and a pleasure in the materiality of glazing, oxidisation and earthenware firing, Brennan's works are made with the poetic licence and sensibility of a painter, rather than a potter, with their unorthodox forms and appendages – including feet, handles and lids – maintaining a sculptural rather than utilitarian demeanour. MD

Angela Brennan
Cup 2012,
Jug with two handles 2013,
Bust with pot 2013

JANE BROWN

Jane Brown was born in Al Ahmadi, Kuwait, and lives and works in Melbourne. She studied photography at the Victorian College of the Arts from 1996 to 1997, holds a Bachelor of Arts from the University of Melbourne and also a Graduate Diploma in Library and Information Management from RMIT University. Her first exhibition, *A Hopeless Taste of Eternity*, was held in Melbourne in 2009, and two years later she held the solo exhibition *Afterlife* at the Ballarat International Foto Biennale. In 2012, Brown's *Australian Gothic* series was included in the exhibition *CCP Declares: On the Nature of Things*, at the Centre for Contemporary Photography, Melbourne.

For *Melbourne Now*, Brown has produced the series *Not Before Time*, 2013. Working with 'almost arcane' film and gelatin silver papers, she explores the transient nature of things, be it her chosen medium or melancholy subjects of decommissioned libraries, steam engines and doomed buildings waiting for the wrecking ball. These photographs prompt feelings of loss and unease, suggesting ghostly imprints rather than hard and fast realities. SvW

Jane Brown
Decommissioned art history library, University of Melbourne 2012–13

Supported by Alistair Hay

LYNDELL BROWN AND CHARLES GREEN WITH JON CATTAPAN

NGVI, Ground Floor, Gallery 29

Working collaboratively since 1989, Lyndell Brown and Charles Green interweave painting and photography to explore cultural representations and archival histories. Blurring the individual hand, Brown/Green create visually and conceptually layered works that overlap and unfold. Jon Cattapan is an equally well-known visual artist who explores political and social representations of the urban environment through paintings of perceptual and narrative complexity. Both Brown/Green (2007) and Cattapan (2008) were commissioned by the Australian War Memorial as Official War Artists, and the three artists are involved in a long-term collaboration.

Brown/Green and Cattapan recently embarked on new works that commence with photographs printed on Duraclear film, overpainted by Cattapan and Brown/Green in turn. This series, *War and Peace*, 2013, explores the aftermath of peacekeeping and war, connecting the Australian landscape to its wider military, media and pop-cultural context. Bringing together their on-site observations, screen culture aesthetics and the image flow of the internet, the pictorial strategies of Brown/Green and Cattapan are not aimed at preserving identity, but rather at suspending spectacle, allowing for close analysis and arrested contemplation. MC

Lyndell Brown
Charles Green
Jon Cattapan
*War and Peace #15:
The Leopard* 2013

TREVOR TURBO BROWN

Mildura-born Trevor Turbo Brown was stolen from his Latje Latje family, grew up in a boys' home in Sydney's west and then lived on the streets where, he claims, animals were his only friends. In 1981 Brown moved to Melbourne and became a celebrity in the Koori community for his boxing at the Fitzroy Stars Gym and breakdancing street performances, which earned him the epithet 'Turbo' after one of the protagonists in the 1984 film *Beat Street*. Brown started painting in 2001 and completed a Diploma of Visual Arts at RMIT University in 2005.

Brown's contribution to *Melbourne Now* comprises a confronting self-portrait, *Last man standing*, 2012, and three spirited paintings of animals in their natural environment symbolic of the artist's vision of his Dreaming Country before it was cleared. Working intuitively with spontaneous brushstrokes, Brown creates joyous impressions of his 'friends' – an owl, a crocodile and two goannas – and captures the verdant landscape with breakdance verve and vivid schematic trees. *Last man standing*, Brown's only known self-portrait, is a moving unmasking of the self, a cry of psychic pain, an exorcism and a dance of freedom. JR

Trevor Turbo Brown
Last man standing 2012

51

JANET BURCHILL AND JENNIFER McCAMLEY

Janet Burchill and Jennifer McCamley have worked collaboratively since the 1980s. Their practice often engages with the legacies of modernism and traverses a wide range of references, from psychoanalysis to film, literature to feminism. It also frequently plays across the boundaries of art and design, sculpture and furniture.

Shields from Papua New Guinea held in the National Gallery of Victoria's collection provided an aesthetic catalyst for the artists to develop an open-ended series of their own 'shields'. *The Belief* includes shields made by Burchill and McCamley between 2004 and 2013. In part, this installation meditates on the form and function of shields from the perspective of a type of reverse ethnography. As the artists explain:

> The shield is an emblematic form ghosted by the functions of attack and defence and characterised by the aggressive display of insignia ... We treat the shield as a perverse type of modular unit. While working with repetition, each shield acts as a carrier or container for different types and registers of content, motifs, emblems and aesthetic strategies. The series as a whole, then, becomes a large sculptural collage which allows us to incorporate a wide range of responses to making art and being alive now.

JD

Janet Burchill
Jennifer McCamley
Oceania communion 2012
(detail)

PENNY BYRNE

Penny Byrne is both a visual artist of repute and a highly respected and sought-after ceramics conservator. Using techniques employed in her conservation work, Byrne creates contentious works of art from recycled mass-produced porcelain figurines and toys. Her often satirical modifications of these coy figurines are not obvious: by tinkering with their kitsch aesthetic Byrne creates a shock of the familiar being used in unexpected ways.

While at first *iProtest*, 2012–13, resembles a display of endearing souvenir-style figurines hanging on a wall, its potency is revealed on closer inspection. Each figurine is personalised with details relating to one of the many conflicts driven by mass protests around the world. Nationalism is referenced by faces painted with flags; acts of violence leave bodies dismembered and bloodied; and the cutest figurines are in fact riot police, wielding guns and dressed as clowns. The omnipresent symbol of Facebook is also ingeniously added to the work. Byrne's crowd of modified figurines explores the way social media has become a significant tool for coordinating protests around the world. **DR**

Penny Byrne
iProtest 2012–13 (detail)

54

DAVID CHESWORTH AND SONIA LEBER

NGVA, Level 2, Gallery 11B

David Chesworth and Sonia Leber have collaborated since 1996 on a series of large-scale installations often utilising the human voice as their principal element, but also involving video, architecture and public participation. The pair's work for *Melbourne Now* is a large-scale high-definition video set in the former *Age* newspaper headquarters on the corner of Spencer and Lonsdale Streets in Melbourne. Speculative and archaeological, the work emerges from this vacant, purpose-built building that once produced the daily news, from its pre-digital technologies and lost modes of communication.

We are printers too, 2013, begins with a lone drummer walking through the abandoned spaces beating rhythmic codes on her drum, evoking announcements and early forms of long-distance communication. Other percussionists inexplicably appear among the silent machines, multiplying the messages, and deaf/blind people 'talk' in sign language about the act of communicating. Exploring the material and sonic by-products of communication, Leber and Chesworth punctuate the work with images of typesetting, telex and the relay mechanisms of a pre-digital telephone exchange and the sounds of morse code and a voice struggling to speak. **DR**

David Chesworth
Sonia Leber
We are printers too 2013 (still)

BORIS CIPUSEV

NGVA, Level 3, Gallery 16C

Boris Cipusev was born in 1988 and has been
working at Arts Project Australia, Melbourne,
since 2007. A prolific and dedicated
practitioner, Cipusev has participated in
numerous group exhibitions in Melbourne
and Sydney since 2007. The artist's beautifully
concise and considered drawings present text
as images. Often employing two words or a
word and number in combination, Cipusev's
works yield both enigmatic juxtapositions
and poetic resonances. For the artist these
words – sometimes names of people he knows
or figures from popular culture – have specific
meaning. Cipusev also draws inspiration
from advertising and signage observed
on his way to and from the studio and from
everyday printed material. His works are often
conceived in series of four parts, completed
in a single session.

   Cipusev's works included in *Melbourne
Now* display the striking and sophisticated
use of contrast between figure and ground
characteristic of his practice, with letters and
words carefully placed and spaced against a
plain white background. Drawn with felt-
tip pen, the works are highly coloured and
precisely delineated, and their clarity and
directness produce an effect both playful
and emphatic. ET

Boris Cipusev
Who next? 2010

Who next?

MAREE CLARKE

Swan Hill–born Maree Clarke lived for a time on Balranald mission and Munatunga mission, Robinvale, before settling in Mildura, and is connected to the traditional lands of the Mutti Mutti, Wamba Wamba, Yorta Yorta and Boonwurrung peoples. Clarke has developed a profound and meditative multidisciplinary practice that re-claims and celebrates precious elements of Aboriginal customary ritual, language and art lost during the colonisation of Victoria.

Clarke's site-specific installation *Ritual and ceremony*, 2013, renders palpable the unconscionable loss and sorrow experienced by Victorian Aboriginal people as a continuing legacy of colonisation. The artist's brooding and poignant photographic images of forty-five men and thirty-eight women bearing ritual markings of mourning create a memorable symbol of collective grief for missing people, stolen Country, lost languages and silenced culture, as well as of resilient survival. Moreover, Clarke's video interviews with the individual subjects enable the frozen portraits to come alive, thereby challenging stereotypes of Victorian Aboriginal people as 'inauthentic', and humanising their experiences. Resonant with the courageous voices of Koori leaders, the installation becomes a healing space inviting intercultural contemplation, sharing and the possibility of reconciliation. JR

Maree Clarke
Men in mourning 2012

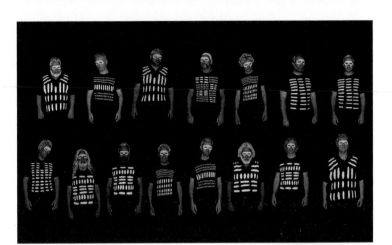

BINDI COLE

NGVA, Ground Floor, Gallery 2A

Bindi Cole is a resilient, ingenious Melbourne-born photographer, curator and new media artist of Wathaurong descent. Cole's early interest in photography was curtailed by a descent into depression and drugs caused by the trauma of her mother's heroin addiction and death from cancer. During a transformative prison term, Cole found Christianity and recaptured her self-belief. Her deeply personal and powerful artistic practice questions the way settler Australians circumscribe and misconstrue contemporary Aboriginal identity and experience.

Cole's *A Wolf in Sheep's Clothing* series, 2012, explores the tension between Christianity and Aboriginality, a conflict between different understandings that has resulted in acts of violence and cultural silencing. The artist has been profoundly changed by the revelation of Jesus, but she struggles with the notion that so many 'wolves in sheep's clothing' ran missions in Victoria that, in the name of God, participated in the decimation of Indigenous culture and languages. The legacy of this difficult history, a longstanding resentment of the atrocities committed under the banner of Christianity, lingers in the Victorian Aboriginal community and throughout the world. **JR**

Bindi Cole
EH5452 2012 (still)

COMMUNITY HALL

NGVI, Ground Floor, Foyer

Melbourne is renowned as being complex, multicultural and multi-layered, qualities the city embraces through its arts, design, fashion, food, sport and cultural events. As a purpose-built space dedicated to Melbourne's diverse communities, *Community Hall* strives to reach beyond the walls of the National Gallery of Victoria to all corners of Melbourne, encouraging conversation and exchange with visitors young and old. For more than one hundred days its circular design, reminiscent of an amphitheatre, will accommodate a wide range of community groups, artist-run initiatives, art and design collectives, students, specialists, performers, collectors, mentors, makers and hobbyists.

Community Hall's rich programming streams will draw out different facets of Melbourne's cultural fabric. Visitors will be treated to a variety of weekly public programs, including Masterclass, Talking Now, Show and Tell, The Menu, *MN* Project, Show-Off, DIY, Guest Who's Next, Melbourne Music and *MN* screenings, all celebrating the diversity of this dynamic city through a schedule of events co-created by you. **ES & YP**

McBride Charles Ryan
Community Hall 2013

Supported by Higgins Coatings

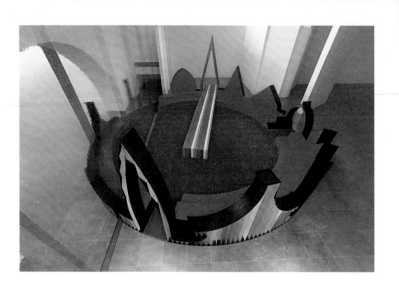

LORRAINE CONNELLY-NORTHEY

NGVA, Ground Floor, Gallery 1A
NGVA, Ground Floor, Gallery 3B

Lorraine Connelly-Northey was born and grew up in Wadi Wadi and Wamba Wamba terrain south of her mother's Waradgerie Country, disconnected from mainsprings of her culture, language and ceremony as a consequence of colonisation. Rather than practising her people's customary art of coil weaving with sedge, Connelly-Northey has forged a dramatic sculptural practice that suits her personal history and hybrid cultural identity. She re-fashions discarded post-industrial materials – the detritus of colonisation – into objects and installations resonant with cultural meaning.

For *Melbourne Now*, Connelly-Northey has constructed two colossal installations, both of which heighten the gulf between pre-contact and postcolonial society. The first, *An O'possum-skin cloak: Blackfella road*, 2011–13, refers to an unsealed road near Swan Hill made from soil taken from culturally sensitive areas containing middens and Aboriginal human remains. This road is boycotted by Connelly-Northey and her family and continues to haunt the artist, as does her memory of visiting and witnessing such decimated sites with her father. Connelly-Northey's second installation, *Vessels*, 2013, a commanding assemblage of giant rusted narbongs (collecting bags) made from incongruous materials, celebrates and memorialises such cultural objects. **JR**

Lorraine Connelly-Northey
An O'possum-skin cloak:
Blackfella road 2011

ALAN CONSTABLE

Alan Constable is a Melbourne-based artist who has been actively practising since 1985. Working principally from the Northcote studios of Arts Project Australia, he has had wideranging critical success in a diversity of media, including pastel on paper, ink on paper, oil on canvas and, more recently, ceramics, and is represented in many national and international collections. Of Constable's diverse works, it is his unique ceramic cameras that stand out as the most significant aspect of his recent practice.

A camera's ability to act as an extension of our eyes and to capture and preserve images renders it a potent instrument. In the case of Constable, this power has particular resonance and added poignancy. The artist lives with profound vision impairment and his compelling, hand-modelled ceramic reinterpretations of the camera – itself sometimes referred to as the 'invented eye' – possess an altogether more moving presence. For *Melbourne Now*, Constable has created a special group of his very personal cameras. DH

Alan Constable
No title (teal SLR with flash)
2013

CONTEMPORARY JEWELLERY

Along with Munich, Amsterdam and other cities, Melbourne is recognised as a leading centre for the production of contemporary jewellery. Established training courses have contributed to this pre-eminence, but the community of local jewellers also includes those who are largely self-taught or whose work has emerged as a result of training in other creative fields. In addition, there are makers whose practice has evolved out of millennia-old cultural traditions, and others who trained overseas and have introduced new ways of working to the local scene.

This diversity of backgrounds among the jewellers represented in *Melbourne Now* is mirrored by the variety of their technical, material and conceptual approaches to making jewellery. Necklaces, bracelets, rings and brooches of precious and semiprecious metals sit alongside others made of resin, porcelain and recycled materials. In this personal and dynamic jewellery merging craft, design, tradition and innovation, the intimate connection between maker and object intersects with that which develops between object and wearer. Melbourne architecture firm Muir Mendes was commissioned to design the contemporary jewellery project for *Melbourne Now*. **KG**

Robert Baines, Roseanne Bartley, Nicholas Bastin, Bin Dixon-Ward, Mark Edgoose, Maureen Faye-Chauhan, Stephen Gallagher, Allona Goren, Jo Hawley, Kirsten Haydon, Marian Hosking, Carlier Makigawa, Sally Marsland, Vicki Mason, David Neale, Tiffany Parbs, Nicole Polentas, Phoebe Porter, Emma Price, Lousje Skala, Blanche Tilden, Meredith Turnbull, Manon van Kouswijk

Allona Goren
play S1 2011

ROSS COULTER

Ross Coulter's practice encompasses photography, filmmaking, sculpture, painting and dance, and is as interesting as it is diverse. Coulter is prolific and his work has been exhibited extensively around Melbourne, from the smallest artist-run initiatives to the National Gallery of Victoria. He has received numerous awards, grants and residencies both locally and internationally.

With *10,000 paper planes – aftermath (1)*, 2011, Coulter encountered Melbourne's intellectual heart, the State Library of Victoria (SLV). Being awarded the Georges Mora Foundation Fellowship in 2010 allowed Coulter to realise a concept he had been developing since he worked at the SLV in the late 1990s. The result is a playful intervention into what is usually a serious place of contemplation. Coulter's paper planes, launched by 165 volunteers into the volume of the La Trobe Reading Room, give physical form to the notion of ideas flying through the building and the mind. This astute work investigates the striking contrast between the strict discipline of the library space and its categorisation system and the free flow of creativity that its holdings inspire in the visitor. HC

Ross Coulter
10,000 paper planes – aftermath (1) 2011
National Gallery of Victoria, Melbourne

ZOË CROGGON

Born in 1989, Zoë Croggon completed a Bachelor of Fine Art (Honours) at the Victorian College of the Arts in 2011, where she received the prestigious ACACIA Art Award. She currently lives and works in Melbourne. Recent group and solo exhibitions in the city include: *Pool*, 2013, *Dodecahedron*, 2012, and *Liquid Archive* at Monash University Museum of Art, 2012.

Combining interests in video, sculpture, architecture, dance and drawing, as well as the open-ended possibilities afforded by re-claiming archival images, Croggon revels in unexpected juxtapositions of forms and textures. Her recent practice has culminated in merging disparate images, found and gathered, into deft and delicate collages. Drawing on personal experiences of studying ballet and dance, Croggon's photo-collages see human forms forced into visual dialogue with images of architecture and natural sites sourced from magazines, newspapers and books. She invests the images with a new currency through the creation of dynamic visual and graphic synergies that have a profound sense of movement, energy and poetry. **MF**

Zoë Croggon
Fonteyn 2012
National Gallery of Victoria, Melbourne

DANIEL CROOKS

New Zealand–born Daniel Crooks has lived and worked in Melbourne for more than twenty years. A multidisciplinary artist, Crooks is well known for his arresting video works in which he masterfully splices and rearranges once-familiar environments into undulating cacophonies of movement. Demonstrating a complex awareness of motion control, physics, design and mathematical code, Crooks's work elevates time to a physical, malleable dimension and challenges our understanding of it as a linear construct.

Commissioned for *Melbourne Now*, Crooks's most recent video work focuses his 'time-slice' treatment on the city's famous laneways. As the camera traces a direct, Hamiltonian pathway through these lanes, familiar surroundings are captured in seamless temporal shifts. Cobblestones, signs, concrete, street art, shadows and people gracefully pan, stretch and distort across our vision, swept up in what the artist describes as a 'dance of energy'. Exposing the underlying kinetic rhythm of all we see, Crooks's work highlights each moment once, gloriously, before moving on, always forward, transforming Melbourne's gritty and often inhospitable laneways into hypnotic and alluring sites. **CR**

Daniel Crooks
A garden of parallel paths
2012 (still)

The commission for *Melbourne Now* is supported by Julie, Michael and Silvia Kantor

GEORGINA CUE

Georgina Cue is known for her diverse practice encompassing large-scale installations which combine embroidery with motifs of film noir and architectural space. Since 2007 she has exhibited regularly in Melbourne, where she lives and works.

The aleph, 2010, is a large installation of embroidery on tapestry canvas that uses trompe l'oeil to create the sense of entering a room. Heavy, patterned drapery and carpets create an atmosphere of times past, and the subdued palette and dark shadows evoke the mystery and suspense of film noir. The work was first shown in an exhibition in Melbourne titled *Indicium*, meaning indication or sign, in which the artist reinterpreted early twentieth-century police photographs of New York crime scenes in embroidery, exploring how mystery and drama imbue everyday objects in these locations. While the melodrama and passion of the crime is absent once the body is removed, the space resonates with the memory of the event, like a stage set after a performance. CC

Georgina Cue
The aleph 2010
National Gallery of Victoria,
Melbourne

DANCE

Independent artists have charged to the forefront of Melbourne's contemporary dance scene in recent years, and now share presentational platforms with the major established dance companies. Solo practice and neo-minimalist aesthetics are hallmarks of local independent work – spectacle is out, normal is in. Is this the result of economic pressure, coupled with an explosion in the numbers of young artists devoted to their practice? Where is dance in Melbourne in 2013, where might it be going and what are the collective values, concerns and philosophies of its practitioners? Does the supreme importance of the individual hold fast in dance as it does in contemporary society and what might this mean for traditional dance?

Melbourne Now's dance program aims to address these questions in a series of discussions and open rehearsals featuring both independent artists and major dance companies. While its focus is on independent practitioners and minimal aesthetics, visually spectacular work is also represented. In addition, the program includes choreography workshops tailored specifically for children. **AH**

Lee Serle
P.O.V. 2013
Dance Massive, Arts House, North Melbourne
Performers/collaborators: James Andrews, Kristy Ayre, Lily Paskas, Lee Serle

The dance program is supported by The Orloff Family Charitable Trust and the Robert Salzer Foundation

JUAN DAVILA

NGVI, Ground Floor, Gallery 29

Juan Davila was born in Santiago, Chile, in 1946, and migrated to Melbourne in 1974. In drawing upon a striking array of art historical and cultural references – religious, modernist and avant-garde art, Latin American folk art traditions, pornographic and pop-cultural motifs and postcolonial and psychoanalytic discourse – Davila has been a leading protagonist in the development of a critical form of post-conceptual painting since the late 1970s, and continues to be at the forefront of cultural and political critique in contemporary art internationally.

More recently, Davila has turned to the genres of landscape and history painting, as well as to portraiture and urban forms, to question the sweep of modernity and colonisation, the rapaciousness of late capitalism and environmental degradation. Recent paintings – such as *After image, Ecran* and *After image, Kreon*, both 2013 – continue to explore indifferent relations between Indigenous, European and migrant communities. In the symbolic and increasingly spectacular forms of advertising and publicity in today's media, Davila identifies a new form of colonisation: of subjectivity itself. With technical virtuosity, his paintings achieve monumental significance – encapsulating beauty and emotion, while invoking society's intolerance of non-commercial enjoyment or desire. MD

Juan Davila
After image, Kreon 2013

CHRISTOPHER DAY

True to the origins of documentary photo-graphy, East Melbourne–born photographer Christopher Day works with everyday objects; his unique use of imagery and choice of subjects, however, turn the genre on its head. Self-taught Day shoots his own source images, carefully selecting objects that resonate with personal memories, before collaging them into psychedelic dreamscapes. The results are surreal, absurd and often humorous, touching on both contemporary and historical narratives and reprocessing artefacts from popular culture. Recent solo exhibitions in Melbourne include *Permanent Deferral*, 2013, *End*, 2012, *After the Breadcrumbs*, 2009, and *A Little Boob*, 2008.

Day's suite of works in *Melbourne Now* are taken from the 2013 *Permanent Deferral* series. The black-and-white photo-collages offer insights into the contemporary media landscape and evoke an almost childlike wonder in the viewer. In the broadest sense, the works offer escapism and the chance to choose your own adventure. **MP**

Christopher Day
Untitled (Permanent deferral)
2013
National Gallery of Victoria, Melbourne

Supported by the Bowness Family Foundation

DESTINY DEACON AND VIRGINIA FRASER

NGVI, Ground Floor, Gallery 27

Destiny Deacon is one of Australia's leading artists, whose work has been presented in major international exhibitions including the prestigious *Documenta 11*, Kassell, 2002. Virginia Fraser is an artist, writer and curator whose practice focuses on film, video and installation using light in various forms. In 2010 Fraser was a Fellow at the National Film and Sound Archive, Canberra.

Adapting the quotidian formats of snapshot photography, home videos, community TV and performance modes drawn from vaudeville and minstrel shows, Deacon's artistic practice is marked by a wicked yet melancholy comedic and satirical disposition. In decidedly lo-fi vignettes, friends, family and members of Melbourne's Indigenous community appear in mischievous narratives that amplify and deconstruct stereotypes of Indigenous identity and national history. For *Melbourne Now*, Deacon and Fraser present a trailer for a film noir that does not exist, a suite of photographs and a carnivalesque diorama. The pair's playful political critiques underscore a prevailing sense of postcolonial unease, while connecting their work to wider global discourses concerned with racial struggle and cultural identity. **MD**

Destiny Deacon
Virginia Fraser
*Blakula's daughter
and Joey* 2011

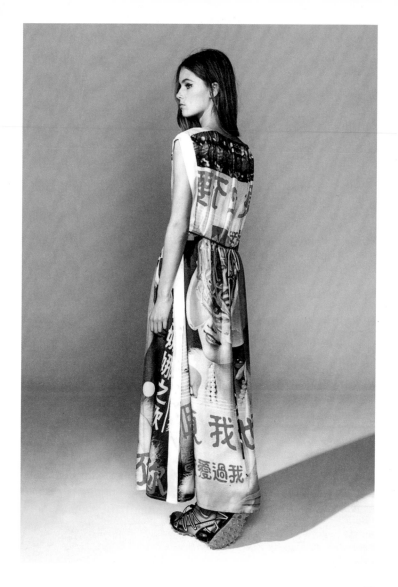

JULIA DEVILLE

Julia deVille was born in New Zealand in 1982 and moved to Melbourne in 2001. While studying gold and silversmithing at NMIT, she completed a mentorship with expert taxidermist Rudy Mineur, and this preservation technique has become a major feature of her work. DeVille believes that taxidermy is a celebration of life, a preservation of something beautiful and a powerful exemplar of the visual language of death.

Informed by a fascination with death, memento mori and Victorian jewellery design, deVille's work relies on traditional techniques and involves a broad range of animals, precious and semiprecious metals and gems. The artist is a vegan and passionate advocate for the fair and just treatment of animals, and only uses animals that have died of natural causes in her work. By examining death in this distinctive way, deVille urges us to consider our own mortality and the beauty of death and remembrance. For *Melbourne Now* she has created an installation titled *Degustation*, 2013, which evokes an ornate Victorian-style dining room, filled with her sculptural pieces and works from the NGV collection. **KS**

Julia deVille
Peter 2012

THE DONKEY'S TAIL
THE DONKEY'S TAIL JNR

NGVA, Level 3, Gallery 18A
NGVI, Level 1 Mezzanine, Gallery 33A

Formed in 2007 by artist John Nixon, The Donkey's Tail is an experimental art-music ensemble featuring a diverse array of artists, musicians and amateur collaborators who perform Nixon's unconventional musical compositions. The group has been prolific in the experimental music scene, releasing more than sixty-five recordings on CD and playing regularly in Melbourne galleries and music venues. Known for their use of homemade instruments constructed from found objects, and for playing orthodox instruments in unorthodox ways, The Donkey's Tail's improvised performances make for engaging and unexpected events. Their recorded material traverses noise instrumentals to songs written by Nixon in folk, spoken word and operatic idioms.

For *Melbourne Now* Nixon's group has conceived an installation encompassing homemade instruments, CDs, photos, paintings, graphic scores, sheet music cover designs, flyers and posters and abstract kinetic videos, all of which invite the audience to explore and discover the group's experimental approach to musical composition, graphic design, instrument-making and performance. *The Donkey's Tail Jnr*, a *Melbourne Now* commission for kids, encourages participants to experiment with sound and create, perform and record their own improvised scores using various musical and sound-making instruments and found objects. **MD**

The Donkey's Tail
Graphic score 21 May 2013
2013

The Donkey's Tail
White guitar 2010

The commission for *Melbourne Now* is supported by *Melbourne Now* Champions the Dewhurst family

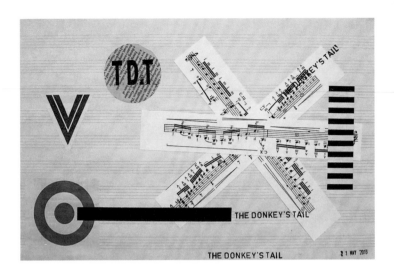

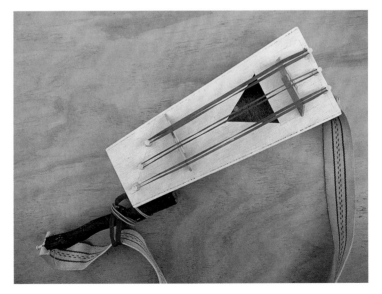

DRAWING NOW

NGVA, Level 3, Gallery 16B

Drawing Now presents drawings from a cross-section of Melbourne artists. As an invited guest artist-curator, I felt it appropriate to take a different approach from that of a museum-based curator. These drawings have been gathered from personal and professional networks and should be seen as a subjective view.

The selection process has been organic, but guided by certain principles. I have not included artists whose primary practice is drawing, but rather focused on those for whom drawing is an allied field for propositions within their work as a whole. I have chosen both abstract and realist art from a wide demographic of artists at different stages in their careers. The works have come from the artists' studios and are not the kind usually offered by them for exhibition, or prioritised in the gallery world. Rather than displaying the works in thematic groupings, I have chosen to present them alphabetically, according to surnames, with a view to emphasising the individuality of each artist's drawing and the diversity of approaches overall. Viewers will find their own links between the works. JN

Artists
A Constructed World, Justin Andrews, John Aslanidis, Damiano Bertoli, Stephen Bram, Nadine Christensen, Renee Cosgrave, Peter Cripps, Domenico de Clario, Leslie Eastman, Anna Finlayson, Emily Floyd, Marco Fusinato, Minna Gilligan, Julia Gorman, Nathan Gray, Melinda Harper, Ry Haskings, Bianca Hester, Raafat Ishak, James Lynch, Taree Mackenzie, Alasdair McLuckie, Andrew McQualter, Dylan Martorell, Ann-Marie May, Victor Meertens, Viv Miller, Callum Morton, Elizabeth Newman, Rose Nolan, Robert Owen, David Palliser, Rosslynd Piggott, Kerrie Poliness, Bryan Spier, Masato Takasaka, Kathy Temin, Robert Vinnecombe, Karl Wiebke, Paul Yore, John Young

Bryan Spier
Untitled 2012

BKS 2012

GEORGE EGERTON-WARBURTON

George Egerton-Warburton's works operate in the realm of chance and unpredictability. Working across video, sculpture, painting, events, performance and installation, Egerton-Warburton often sets up the conditions for an uncontrollable reaction to take place. He has exhibited widely in Australia and New Zealand in recent years and is currently a studio resident at Gertrude Contemporary, Melbourne.

In Egerton-Warburton's single-take film *Why are you wearing athletic gear if you're not playing any sport today? (Melbourne: Run Artist Run)*, 2013, viewers are escorted past landmarks of Melbourne's artist-run community. Glimpses of the protagonist's shoes in the footage reflect contemporary trends in Melbourne's artistic community which conflate urban fashion, criminality, yoga culture and post-London riot footwear to articulate radical chic. The film concludes with the camera being placed on a tripod in the space where it is later installed. Completing a cycle from three-dimensional to two-dimensional space and back again, the resulting work is an examination of the awkward moral balance in nature and the expanded notion of video as well as structuralist filmmaking techniques. **JW**

George Egerton-Warburton
Steaming ties 2013

TAMA tk FAVELL

Contemporary printmaker Tama tk Favell works mainly in linocut and other forms of relief printing. The artist was born in Ōtepoti/Dunedin, Aotearoa/New Zealand, and moved to Melbourne in 2001. He studied printmaking at the Victorian College of the Arts, receiving a Bachelor of Fine Art (Honours) in 2010.

Favell's *Pacific Transformer* series of linocuts, 2009–13, for *Melbourne Now* explores and develops the idea that male spiritual identity can be expressed through iconographic tattooing, creating a cultural means of gender transition as an alternative and/or addition to the Western medical model. His use of mulberry paper is a tribute to and continuation of the use of tapa cloth (beaten mulberry bark) at times of transition throughout the Pacific. This powerful body of work is an account of the negotiation and navigation required to live between worlds. It is about moving between forms, changing form, the integration of self and culture and being *takatapui*, queer/transgender in a culturally Pacific sense. Favell's ultimate vision is for his imagery to be applied to his skin. **SB**

Tama tk Favell
Pacific transformer 3
2009–13
National Gallery of Victoria, Melbourne

EMILY FLOYD

Melbourne-born artist Emily Floyd holds a Bachelor of Arts from Swinburne University of Technology, and a Bachelor of Fine Art (Sculpture) from RMIT University. Since 2001 she has presented numerous solo exhibitions, including at the Bendigo Art Gallery; Monash University Museum of Art, Melbourne; and the Museum of Contemporary Art, Sydney, among others.

Floyd's prints and sculptures explore the history of pedagogical play, employing it as a framework for investigations into literature, typography, protest, public art and the legacy of modernism. Her work incorporates bold colour and geometrical forms referencing early modernist movements and collectives, such as De Stijl, the Bauhaus and Russian Constructivism. Floyd's work in *Melbourne Now, Students in dissent*, 2013, is a collaborative screen-printing project with Stewart Russell, Warren Taylor and students from Monash Art Design and Architecture. The project was generated through Floyd's research into the history and legacy of radical student organisations based at Monash University during the 1960s and 1970s. The group worked together to reproduce nine political posters from the archive of former Monash Labor Club activist Ken Mansell. **PK**

Emily Floyd, Stewart Russell, Warren Taylor and students from Monash Art Design and Architecture: Joshua Aucutt, Melissa Coombs, Jessica Dixon, Paul Failla, Jacqui Gordon, Belinda Hosford, Jessica Hoskin, Samantha Liu, Georgia Munn, Paul Sin, Kimberley Soda, Vivian Taing, Nancy Truong, Louise Walker, Jessica Williams
Students in dissent 2013 (detail)

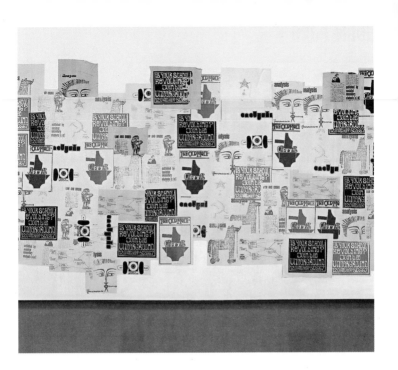

103

JUAN FORD

In his work, Juan Ford often pursues themes of transformation and discord between man and nature. While best known for realist paintings of people, landscape, nature, light and shadow, in recent times Ford has branched out and created installations incorporating photography. The artist lives in Melbourne and graduated from RMIT University in 1998. He has exhibited extensively throughout Australia in solo and group shows, and has work in the NGV collection.

Separation, alignment and cohesion are three interrelated concepts applied by scientists in their attempt to understand the behaviour of flocking birds. For his *Melbourne Now* commission for kids *You, me and the flock*, 2013, Ford investigates how this behaviour relates to human beings by inviting viewers of all ages to add birds to a flock that inhabits a panoramic sky-scape. Each bird added changes the flock's shape and movement as it grows and becomes overpopulated, resulting in some birds breaking away to form another configuration. With this playful installation, Ford poses challenging questions about human behaviour, highlighting our interaction with precious natural habitats. **DHi**

Juan Ford
You, me and the flock 2013
(detail)

Supported by *Melbourne Now* Champions the Dewhurst family

LOUISE FORTHUN

For the past three decades, Louise Forthun has reworked the urban landscape to the point of abstraction. The artist uses stencil painting processes to pile layers of architectural representations on top of one another, enveloping the viewer in a hypnotic vision of the contemporary metropolis. Since she began exhibiting in Melbourne in the 1990s, Forthun has sustained an ongoing investigation into critical abstraction through her work. She describes herself as 'a visual artist who makes paintings that explore abstraction's objective as well as non-objective dimensions'.

For *Melbourne Now*, Forthun contributes one of her most ambitious works to date – a portrait of Melbourne entitled *Bright light*, 2011. More than five metres in length, Forthun's representation of her home city interweaves details drawn from an aerial plan of Melbourne with more familiar representations of its landmarks to create an immersive spatial construction that echoes the frenetic energy of its source. LC

Louise Forthun
Bright light 2011

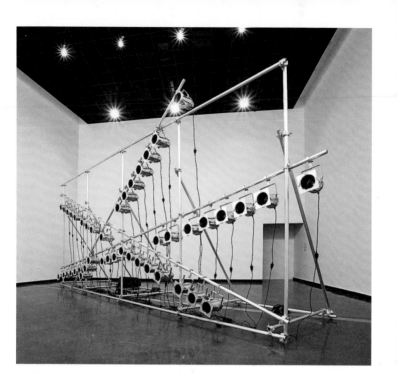

TONY GARIFALAKIS

NGVA, Level 3, Gallery 17A

Through his expansive art practice, Tony Garifalakis calls into question the authority and veracity of political, social, religious and artistic institutions. Working across photography, collage, sculpture and installation, his works uncover connections between consumer culture and control society, enacting an emancipatory subversion of commodities and consumer iconography.

In *Melbourne Now* Garifalakis presents *Mutually Assured Destruction*, 2010–13, a series of collages that make use of denim and mine its rich cultural connotations. These new works juxtapose loaded political and corporate imagery with cute and benign clip art. By confusing the disparate images, the works collapse any power they might have in other contexts. The collages describe causal links between corporate culture of the First World and religious fundamentalist militarism. Garifalakis reveals denim as a material paradox: at once a stylistic representation of gang and outlaw cultures, and a billion-dollar mainstream global fashion industry. **SM**

Tony Garifalakis
East River 2012

STARLIE GEIKIE

Hovering somewhere in the realms of drawing, painting, textile design, installation and craft, Melbourne-based artist Starlie Geikie's works resist easy classification. Since completing a Master of Fine Art at RMIT University in 2002, Geikie has developed a unique visual language that mines a rich archive of material and historical references, from feminist literary fiction and modernist interior design to Shaker furniture and the collages of Hannah Höch.

Combining formalist concerns with an atmosphere redolent of the 1970s, Geikie's recent works combine references to the Bauhaus weavings of Gunta Stölz and Anni Albers, the visionary geometric drawings of Emma Kunz and the colourfield paintings of Morris Louis, as well as experimental textile dying, Amish quilts and the aesthetics of nautical knot craft. While making her works, Geikie often imagines them in certain historical or cultural settings, such as the modernist interior of a Geoffrey Bawa house, or sitting on a Charlotte Perriand chair. As she explains: 'I think of [my works] ... in the way an art director would. They become props in interior shoots or 1970s movies'. JD

Starlie Geikie
Moors 2013

MIRA GOJAK

NGVA, Level 3, Gallery 18B

Mira Gojak completed a Bachelor of Science, majoring in psychology and zoology, at the University of Adelaide in 1984, before undertaking a Bachelor of Fine Art in painting at the Victorian College of the Arts, Melbourne, graduating in 1992. Gojak's practice encompasses drawing and sculpture and, since 1994, she has exhibited widely in a range of solo and group exhibitions, both locally and abroad. In 2005 Gojak was awarded the prestigious Maddocks Art Prize. She currently lives and works in Melbourne.

With *Transfer station 2*, 2011, Gojak creates a sculptural work of unfurling, freewheeling loops, shaky erratic lines and clusters of blossoming tangles that appears like a drawing suspended in space. A high-keyed palette of cobalt blues, soft pinks and fluorescent yellows activates heavier blackened thickets that punctuate perspectives of uninterrupted space. Suspended from the ceiling by a single line, Gojak's sculpture is a not-quite-settled-upon Venn diagram. Its openness is held still in a moment, together with all the scribbled-out mistakes, digressions and exclusions, stalling or directing the movement and exchange circulating around the forms. JC

Mira Gojak
Transfer station 2 2011 (detail)

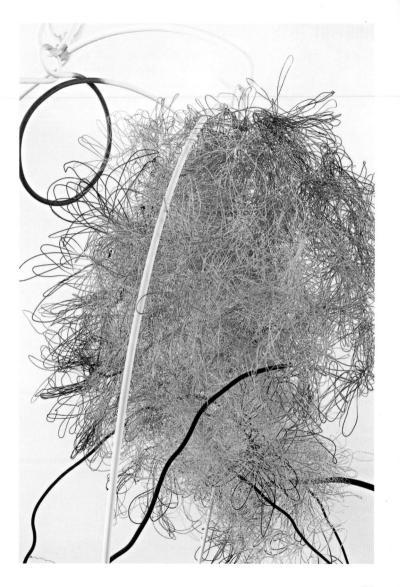

117

AGATHA GOTHE-SNAPE

NGVI, Ground Floor, Gallery 22

Incorporating text, colour and space, the work of Agatha Gothe-Snape considers physical, emotional and historical responses to the reception of art. Through her conceptually driven and cross-disciplinary practice the artist aims to develop new conversations around institutional, social and historical discourse while maintaining an ongoing dialogue between audiences and the social world. Often taking form as performances, endlessly looped Microsoft PowerPoint presentations, visual scores, posters and collaboratively produced art objects, Gothe-Snape's works are regularly made in cooperation with other artists, performers, dancers and the audience.

Drawing influence from concrete poetry, colourfield painting and the emergence of internet art, *Powerpoints*, 2008–13, is an ongoing series of unlimited-edition digital works that utilise the basic communicative tools of Microsoft PowerPoint. Established in 2008 and conceived as a lifelong project, Gothe-Snape's slide shows are created sporadically, manifested in a private and contractual email correspondence between the artist and subscribers. Since its inception, Gothe-Snape has produced a total of twenty-four works in the series, including two new instalments made especially for *Melbourne Now*. This is the first time the series has been shown its entirety. **AR & GJ**

Agatha Gothe-Snape
Powerpoints 2008–13 (detail)

TODAY

EVERYTHING ELSE

FEELINGS

BIG OPINIONS

STAND DOWN SNAKE CHARMERS

SIGN AND DELIVER

FALSE

NOW

ELIZABETH GOWER

Since the 1970s Elizabeth Gower has created and exhibited intricate collages, composed from detritus of everyday life which she carefully selects and arranges in rhythmic and geometric permutations. Gower has exhibited widely throughout Australia and overseas in numerous solo and group shows, and has curated a number of exhibitions. She is a lecturer at the University of Melbourne and the Victorian College of the Arts, and is currently completing a PhD at Monash University.

The first version of this work was displayed recently in an exhibition, curated by Gower, that explored the appropriation and use of urban detritus as a visual art strategy by a variety of Melbourne artists. Further developed for *Melbourne Now*, Gower's contribution now comprises 150 circular components, each made up of tea-bag tags, price tags and elements cut from junk mail catalogues, which colonise the wall like a galaxy of vibrant constellations. Akin to the light from long-dead stars, the familiar ephemera, which is usually thrown out, recycled or composted, now serves a new purpose and takes on a mesmeric, formal beauty. **AB**

Elizabeth Gower
150 rotations 2013 (detail)

GREATEST HITS

Greatest Hits is a collective comprised of artists Gavin Bell, Jarrah de Kuijer and Simon McGlinn. Formed in Melbourne in 2008, the group produces a variety of work through outsourcing and minimal interventions as a form of information management. Interested in the gathering speed and increase of communication, the collective's focus is on a culture created by this environment, characterised by immediacy, instinct and renewal. Greatest Hits have exhibited in various solo and group shows both internationally and locally, including *Untitled*, The Projects, Melbourne, and *FX*, Centre for Contemporary Photography, Melbourne, both 2013.

In *Untitled*, 2012, Greatest Hits brings together two well-known tropes: the Japanese beckoning cat 'maneki-neko' and the representation of the black cat as an ill omen. The common associations of these icons – that of inviting good and bad fortunes respectively – set the stage for a pseudo-logical argument that attempts to rid itself of meaning. Taking its cue from the voiding effects of exposure to excessive information, the work engages with the language of surface culture, in which depth and focus is increasingly replaced by montage and movement. **JD & JW**

Greatest Hits
Untitled 2012

HELEN GROGAN, SHELLEY LASICA AND ANNE-MARIE MAY

NGVI, Level 3, Gallery 39A

The collaborative practice of Helen Grogan, Shelley Lasica and Anne-Marie May brings choreography and movement into the gallery context, mediated by layers of projection, sound and objects. Sharing interests in process, collaboration and intermedial practices, the artists draw on credentials in varied art forms: Grogan studied philosophy, choreography and art curatorship and since 2003 has exhibited as an installation artist; Lasica is a choreographer and dancer whose work is characterised by cross-disciplinary collaborations and the presentation of dance in various spatial contexts; and May studied painting, her twenty-five-year practice concerned with the interplay between different materials and processes.

The installation *INSIDE VIANNE AGAIN*, 2013, continues a collaborative project exploring the context of performance and its presentation. For *Melbourne Now*, dancers Deanne Butterworth, Timothy Harvey, Jo Lloyd and Bonnie Paskas were recorded performing the work *VIANNE*, choreographed by Lasica, in the NGV gallery space. This footage is projected back onto the space itself, including sculptural objects. Thus the work creates slippages between layers of representation, time, architecture and bodies – of both the performers and viewers who navigate the space. LC

Helen Grogan
Shelley Lasica
Anne-Marie May
INSIDE VIANNE AGAIN 2013

MICHELLE HAMER

Michelle Hamer is an architect-turned-textile artist whose work interrogates the vernacular of Melbourne's civic landscape. Since 2005 Hamer has produced small-scale needlepoint tapestries that reference forms of text and signage in the urban environment. From road signs to graffiti to billboards and advertising, Hamer's interest is in language and meaning, and her tapestries are a kind of social cartography. Journeying around specific sites, Hamer first takes endless snapshots before sifting and sorting through them, formulating a visual hypothesis which she later executes in material form.

Hamer's contribution to *Melbourne Now* pairs works referencing local signage, *Blame and punish the individual*, 2013, and *Can't*, 2013, with three earlier tapestries from her American series *I Send Mixed Messages*, 2013. While the contrasting palettes and particular nuances of typography, built architecture and native vegetation point to specific times and places, when amplified and dislocated Hamer's chosen texts suggest a more universal narrative of perplexity and turmoil. The artist describes these powerful distillations as 'revealing the small in-between moments that characterise everyday life'. **DW**

Michelle Hamer
Can't 2013

TREAHNA HAMM

NGVA, Ground Floor, Gallery 1A

Melbourne-born Treahna Hamm was disconnected from her Yorta Yorta family in early infancy, but grew up in her ancestral lands Dhungala (the Murray River), upstream from Echuca. In 2001 Hamm returned to Barmah in order to trace her living connection to this Country. She participated in a coil-weaving workshop led by Yvonne Koolmatrie and embarked on *didjirri* (deep listening) in communion with female elders. Hamm's subsequent woven fibre and sculptural work has issued from a resolve to re-claim the cultural stories, objects, designs and philosophy previously hidden from her.

Hamm's work for *Melbourne Now* is a body of breastplates that subverts and transforms objects of disquieting and ambivalent status made by colonisers as a way of labelling, rewarding and pacifying their colonised subjects. These deep crescent-shaped objects reference metal breastplates, such as that of 'King Billy' (William Barak), which belonged to Hamm's Indigenous family. The intricate curvilinear motifs incised on the breastplates express her people's resilient culture and indelible connection to Dhungala Country, which the tide of history cannot wash away. JR

Treahna Hamm
*Cummeragunjah
breastplate 2* 2005
National Gallery of Victoria,
Melbourne

BRENT HARRIS

Brent Harris was born in New Zealand and has lived and worked in Melbourne since 1981. A painter who also works extensively in the prints and drawings media, Harris is well known for his explorations of human subjectivity in images that hover between figuration and abstraction. His work has undergone several radical shifts over the course of his career, and an important new direction was signalled by the group of monotypes begun in 2012. Intimate and experimental, these brooding nocturnal scenes evoke a fantastic nether world of supernatural creatures and ageing figures inspired by the artist's reflection upon the psychology of death.

Since Edgar Degas's time, the monotype has been prized by artists as a medium particularly suited to improvisation. In *the fall*, 2012, included in *Melbourne Now*, Harris has exploited this to the full, intuitively reworking and resolving his imagery on the plates before printing them. The enigmatic imagery in Harris's monotypes – tumbling figures, ghoulish heads, skulls, inky skies and dark, mysterious bodies of water – speaks to our deepest fears concerning mortality and the absurdity of the human condition. **CL**

Brent Harris
the fall (no. 9) 2012
National Gallery of Victoria,
Melbourne

PONCH HAWKES

Ponch Hawkes was born in Melbourne in 1946. She began to photograph in the 1970s and held her first exhibition in Melbourne in 1976. Since then Hawkes has held numerous solo shows, including *Relatively Speaking: The Family in Words and Pictures*, Centre for Contemporary Photography, Melbourne, 1998, and *Generations*, National Gallery of Victoria, 1989. More recent one-person exhibitions include *Seeing Is Not Understanding*, Horsham Regional Art Gallery, 2009, and *Risk*, Monash Gallery of Art, Melbourne, 2005.

For *Melbourne Now* Hawkes has produced a new body of work, *Drawing the Line*, 2013, that examines an aspect of how we interact with the natural environment in an urban setting. In a local park, a place of daily retreat for the artist, Hawkes encountered the phenomenon of 'tree tagging'. Her initial response was one of profound shock and disgust at the deliberate defacing of native trees. There is an aspect of premeditated violence in these acts, yet Hawkes subsumes the aggressors' marks into redemptive images as the trees shed their bark and transform the tags. SvW

Ponch Hawkes
TAGS # 4 2013

SIRI HAYES

Siri Hayes was born in Melbourne in 1977. She completed a Bachelor of Fine Art and a Graduate Diploma of Visual Art at the Victorian College of the Arts in 1998 and 2001 respectively. Hayes has held positions as a photography lecturer and technician, and is currently a lecturer in photomedia at Monash University, Melbourne. Since 2000 her work has been included in group exhibitions throughout Australia, as well as in Finland, France, Japan and Poland.

Hayes's work often addresses environmental themes within art historical conventions. In her photographs for *Melbourne Now*, she cites the conventions of the French Impressionist painters, who painted their subjects en plein air (outdoors), and the Romantic landscape paintings of Caspar David Friedrich. Here, modern 'explorers' and 'wanderers' paint and make photographs in a contemporary environment. The environment, however, is one of decay: devastated by fire, littered with tree stumps and broken branches and its native vegetation replaced by introduced, harvested plantation timber. By adapting historical painting conventions to a modern setting, Hayes draws attention to the changing condition of the contemporary landscape. **PD**

Siri Hayes
Wanderer above a sea of images 2013

ANDREW HAZEWINKEL

Multidisciplinary artist Andrew Hazewinkel was born in Melbourne in 1965 and has exhibited widely in Australia and abroad for more than ten years. His practice includes photography, video, installation and sculpture. Hazewinkel's work draws its influence from a wide range of sources, the most pertinent and apparent being anthropology, archaeology and other recordings of history. This is not only evident in the subjects of his work, but also in the techniques and methods he employs, which in the past have seen him take a sculptural approach to collage, often incorporating ready-made objects.

In his works *Material collision (Staring together at the stars) #1, #2,* and *#3, 2013,* Hazewinkel's archival explorations address history, time, materiality and process. These large works on carborundum sandpaper re-contextualise and, in a strange way, revive three forgotten objects of antiquity. Despite not being the original, three-dimensional objects, these documentations are nonetheless weighted with history. Hazewinkel's interpretation and re-documentation of these perhaps forgotten objects bridges a gap between the present and the past, and transforms our experience and study of history, modernity and contemporaneity. **NA**

Andrew Hazewinkel
Material collision (Staring together at the stars) #1
2013 (detail)

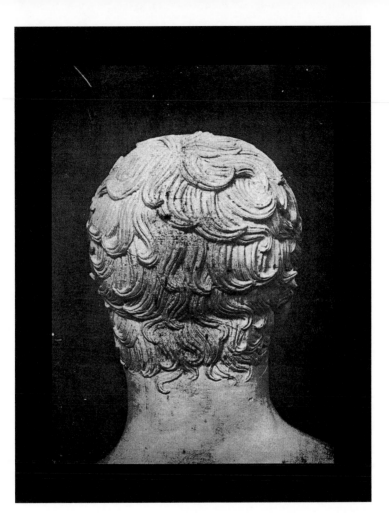

BIANCA HESTER

Since the early 2000s, Melbourne artist Bianca Hester has worked across installation, sculpture, video, writing, sound and collaborative disciplines to create action-and-response performances. Her projects typically observe junctures between different social conditions, sites and moments in time, and involve architectural and sculptural interventions. By actively engaging with (rather than against) unpredictable forces, Hester aims to heighten the spatial and bodily awareness of both the performer and the viewer. Her actions are preserved and represented through documentary photographs and film.

Hoops: sound tests, performances, documents (2011–13), 2013, is an exploration of abstract sound and repeated gesture, produced by rolling and spiralling steel hoops along concrete, floorboards and pavement. Composed as open-ended events, Hester's ongoing *Hoops* projects have previously been presented in car parks, public squares, community clubs and urban laneways – all civic spaces – but never in a museum context. By staging a *Hoops* performance within the National Gallery of Victoria, the artist negotiates a new set of criteria, acting in response to the wider conceptual narrative of *Melbourne Now*. GJ

Bianca Hester
Sound test with hoops in Federation Square, Melbourne 2011 (still)
performance component of the project *A world fully accessible by no living being* 2011

CHRISTOPHER LG HILL

NGVA, Level 2, Gallery 11C

Christopher LG Hill has been involved in various projects at both artist-run and institutional spaces across Melbourne, including co-directing the artist-run initiative Y3K (2009–11), editing the annual periodical *Endless Lonely Planet* and curating the *Third/Fourth Melbourne Artist Facilitated Biennial* at Margaret Lawrence Gallery in 2013. Engaging with concepts of psychology, sociology and gestural poetics, Hill's idiosyncratic practice examines the relationships between people, freedom and objects. The artist describes his work as 'embracing anarchist ideas within interpersonal relationships, materialised through free intellectual property, publications, performance, object dialogs and gestural interactions'. He often works with other artists to create critical and open responses to his performances and installations.

Hill's *Form free temporal groupings*, 2013, is an aesthetically lo-fi installation that involves collaborations with young artists and designers ffiXXed, Tahi Moore, Virginia Overell, Alex Vivian, Hugh Egan Westland, Annie Wu and Ben Tankard, among others. A range of impromptu performances, including readings and discussion groups, form part of this work, allowing the artist, his collaborators and the public to explore interactions between installation and broader artistic practices. **AR**

Christopher LG Hill
Free feudal barter store 2013
installation view, Gertrude
Contemporary, Melbourne

MARK HILTON

Since graduating from the Victorian College of the Arts in 1999, Mark Hilton has exhibited both locally and internationally in contemporary art spaces and artist-run initiatives. Working across drawing, painting, sculpture and video, the artist approaches the psychology of collective decision-making to determine and question 'normal' behavioural codes.

dontworry, 2013, included in *Melbourne Now*, is the most ambitious and personal work Hilton has made to date. A dark representation of events the artist witnessed growing up in suburban Melbourne, this wall-based installation presents an unnerving picture of adolescent mayhem and bad behaviour. Extending across nine intricately detailed panels, each corresponding to a formative event in the artist's life, *dontworry* can be understood as a deeply personal memoir that explores the transition from childhood to adulthood, and all the complications of this experience. Detailing moments of violence committed by groups or mobs of people, the installation revolves around Hilton's continuing fascination with the often indistinguishable divide between truth and myth. **AR**

Mark Hilton
dontworry 2013

MATT HINKLEY

Matt Hinkley is best known for small-scale works with intricate patterns and finely rendered graphic details. Since graduating from the Queensland College of Art, Brisbane, in 2000, the Melbourne-based artist has adopted a pragmatic approach to making art, often using simple means and humble materials, including various found objects, newspaper and graph paper and, more recently, plaster, silicon and polymer clays. Straddling the disciplines of drawing, collage and sculpture, Hinkley's works combine an understated aesthetic and a DIY sensibility to establish new trajectories for non-objective abstraction.

Hinkley's most recent works comprise a series of small plaster objects inscribed with dazzling patterns and intricate relief-like qualities. Developed from processes previously used by the artist to produce a series of miniature polymer clay sculptures, these latest works demand careful observation, revealing fragments of highly detailed abstract 'drawings' hand-etched with painstaking precision. From a distance, these small sculptures reveal subtle shifts in form, tone and texture. Up close, their complex surface details suggest infinite expressive possibilities. JD

Matt Hinkley
Untitled 2013

HOTHAM STREET LADIES

NGVA, Ground Floor, Foyer

Hotham Street Ladies (HSL) is a group of five women whose work is rooted in their experiences of sharing a run-down but much-loved house in Hotham Street, Collingwood. The collective's members are Cassandra Chilton, Molly O'Shaughnessy, Sarah Parkes, Caroline Price and Lyndal Walker. Their practice embraces themes of home life, feminism and craft and explores how collaborative participation in, and contemporising of, these activities creates a distinct cultural community. Their work's innovative combination of humour and contemporary critique with nostalgic or familiar elements makes it appealing to a wide audience. Often thought of in terms of dysfunction, the share house in their hands becomes a site of creativity, cooperation and overindulgence.

Food is a constant presence in HSL's work, from recipe swap meets, street art and public art commissions to controversial cake entries in the Royal Melbourne Show. For *Melbourne Now* the group take baking and icing to a whole new level. Their installation *At home with the Hotham Street Ladies*, 2013, transforms the foyer of The Ian Potter Centre: NGV Australia into an icing-bombed domestic wonderland. Their commission for kids invites children and families to photograph themselves within one of the scenes from HSL's icing- and lolly-encrusted share house. **KS**

Hotham Street Ladies
Luxury with leftovers 2013

LOU HUBBARD

NGVA, Level 3, Gallery 18B

Lou Hubbard began her career in film and television, and has exhibited extensively in Australia and overseas since 2000. In a process that is lo-fi, compulsive and absurd, Hubbard manipulates materials in accordance with a set of strict, self-governed rules. The artist pushes, pulls and provokes everyday objects in video works of these actions as well as in sculptural assemblages. The resulting works are awkwardly balanced arrangements that present illogical narratives about sentiment and pathos in human experience and hint at the layers of anxiety we secretly negotiate on a daily basis.

For *Melbourne Now*, Hubbard presents *EYE OPS*, 2013, a cluster of related video works developed during her recent Australia Council–funded residency in Barcelona. These videos show Hubbard performing a series of actions upon eyeballs created – in keeping with her absurdist palette – from marshmallow. Hubbard interrogates the anthropomorphic and physical qualities of the objects, rolling and compressing, slicing and rearranging them, to display a vicissitude of substance that alternates between humour and gruesomeness. **LC**

Lou Hubbard
EYE OPS 2013 (still) from
Series 1: Spectacle

EYE OPS 2013 (still) from
Series 2: Operations

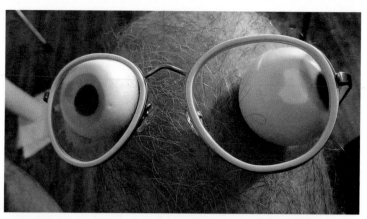

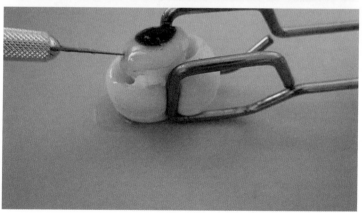

SHANE HULBERT

Shane Hulbert was born in Sydney in 1971 and moved to Melbourne two years later. He completed a PhD in Fine Art at RMIT University in 2012 and currently lectures in photography at his alma mater. He has exhibited widely in Australia and abroad since 1997. Hulbert's work, which has its roots in the tradition of landscape photography, is focused on unique aspects of Australian landscape, identity and culture.

Recently Hulbert has explored the expression of a collective national identity through distinct and now-popular iconography that illustrates his fascination with the connections between place, history and culture. In *Melbourne Now* the artist is showing five photographs from his recent *Import/ Export* series, 2011–13, that celebrate the icons and myths that help define Australian identity. Featuring a combination of locations, personalities and 'larrikin' humour, the photographs consider ways in which foreign locations encapsulate the idea of Australia. The series also responds to the evolving assimilation of imported cultural icons and their relationship to contemporary Australia. **NA**

Shane Hulbert
Spirit of Bengali, Grampians
2013

BRENDAN HUNTLEY

Brendan Huntley was born in Melbourne, in 1982. His first solo exhibition, *End to End*, was held in 2005. In 2013 his work was exhibited in *Primavera* at the Museum of Contemporary Art, Sydney. Huntley revels equally in painting and sculpture. He breaks every rule associated with traditional ceramic techniques and makes paintings that appear to be bursting out of their frames. Through the moulding and distortion of clay, Huntley creates distinctive ceramic sculptures that reconsider conventional notions of the vessel. His experimentation with the medium, such as the grafting of terracotta and porcelain clays and his painterly treatment of slips and glazes, results in startlingly original works.

Exhibited in *Melbourne Now* is a selection of Huntley's figurative sculptural forms that reflect his interest in historical and ethnographic collections. The artist's diverse approach to each form's materiality, shape and scale grants the figures their own strong character and unique persona. Huntley's quirky, engaging forms convey his will to connect with and manipulate figurative and narrative traditions. **BR**

Brendan Huntley
Untitled 2010–11
National Gallery of Victoria, Melbourne

ELIZA HUTCHISON

Melbourne-based artist Eliza Hutchison was born in South Africa in 1965. She completed a Bachelor of Film and Theatre Studies at the University of New South Wales, Sydney, in 1988, a Bachelor of Fine Art in sculpture and photography at RMIT University, Melbourne, in 1992, and in 1994 graduated from the Sydney College of the Arts with an Honours degree in Fine Art.

Continuing the artist's interrogation of the material and illusionistic properties of photographs and the relationship between photography and psychology, works from Hutchison's *Kewpie and the Corn Idol* series, 2010–13, see her distorting, shredding and recomposing images generated from identical movie posters from the *Twilight* teen movie series. Abstracted at first glance, hints of the familiar are occasionally revealed – profiles of Hollywood actors emerge from the strips and shreds of papers. In the adjoining sculptural piece *Busto I*, 2009–10, Hutchison fashions more shredded poster strips atop a plywood plinth resembling a pagan corn idol. There is a conflation between the ideas of nature and culture which becomes evident as the images appear as re-figured and transmuted organic matter. **MF**

Eliza Hutchison
No 8 2010

RORY HYDE

NGVI, Ground Floor, Federation Court

Rory Hyde's work in architecture encompasses design, research, broadcasting and building. Recently returned to Melbourne after four years in Amsterdam, Hyde is co-host of *The Architects*, on Triple R radio, Melbourne, whose project *Architecture on the Air* was presented at the 2012 Venice Architecture Biennale. Hyde completed a PhD on emerging models of architectural practice enabled by new technologies, and recently published *Future Practice: Conversations from the Edge of Architecture* (2012). His work actuates an expanded conception of architectural practice through dialogue, collaboration and experimental architectural forms which activate space as a catalyst for social engagement.

Hyde's project for *Melbourne Now* builds upon his involvement with the celebrated *Bucky bar*, 2011, an unsolicited architectural form developed in association with DUS Architects in Rotterdam. His commission for Federation Court at NGV International is a space for social encounter, impromptu events, performances and broadcasts, encompassing a geodesic dome and weather balloon in reference to Roy Grounds's pole-framed geodesic dome at Penders, New South Wales, c.1966, among other art and architectural precedents, from Buckminster Fuller and Olafur Eliasson to the legendary Colorado artists' commune of 1965, Drop City. **MD**

Rory Hyde (designer)
Tobias Pond (project architect)
Jon Anderson (structural engineer)
Bin dome proposal 2013

Supported by the Loti and Victor Smorgon Fund

156

RICARDO IDAGI

NGVA, Ground Floor, Gallery 3A

Multidisciplinary artist and musician Ricardo Idagi is a risk-taker who dares to dream and defy convention. Idagi spent much of his early life on Mer (Murray Island), was educated in Townsville and travelled as an itinerant musician before moving to Melbourne in 1997. Much of his formative work crystallises a deep reverence for Meriam customary art and culture. His art also unashamedly confronts personal trauma, racism, linguicide and irrevocable loss caused by white colonisation and the Christianisation of the Torres Strait.

Idagi's *False evidence appearing real*, 2013, is a disarmingly honest examination of his negative self-image, conceived as a ceramic self-portrait of startling likeness. To guard against portraying himself as a swollen-headed, narcissistic artist, Idagi literally 'puts shit' on himself by placing a galah on his head that gazes in a mirror and leaves droppings below. Like Idagi's other ceramic portraits, this work projects his innermost fears and past experience of child abuse, proselytisation and unconscionable racism. In working the clay, Idagi exorcises the constant taunts and resultant shame that have scarred his sense of self, and resists his demonisation. **JR**

Ricardo Idagi
False evidence appearing real 2013
National Gallery of Victoria, Melbourne

159

LUCY IRVINE

Lucy Irvine emigrated from Scotland to Melbourne in 2003 and in 2008 undertook a Master of Fine Arts at the Victorian College of the Arts. During her studies she developed a sculptural practice that explores her experiences and memory of landscape. The artist's expansive organic works are made from industrial materials, woven incrementally and secured by tiny cable-tie 'stitches'. The forms of the enveloping structures are driven by process and articulate a tension between order and chaos.

For *Melbourne Now* Irvine has constructed a large site-specific work at The Ian Potter Centre: NGV Australia, *Before the after*, 2013, which establishes a dialogue with the gallery building, its architecture and the temporality of the exhibition. Spilling out across the floor, the serpentine form is an interruption of the order of things, a writhing obsidian mass that clings to the interior of the building. At the same time the work is a nuanced meditation on the nature of surfaces and skin. Irvine's iterative practice argues for value in the gestural, and proposes the act of making as a form of knowledge. **DW**

Lucy Irvine
The traveller 2010 (detail)

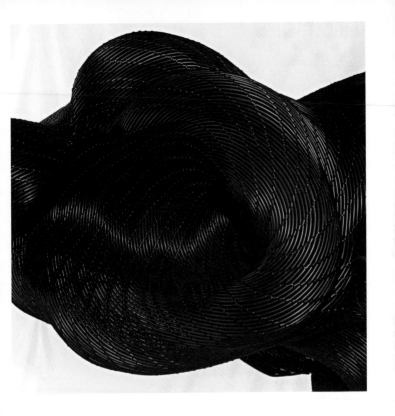

RAAFAT ISHAK

Born in Egypt, Raafat Ishak immigrated to Australia in 1982. He completed a Bachelor of Fine Art at the Victorian College of the Arts and is currently undertaking a PhD at Monash University. His practice encompasses painting, sculpture, drawing and installation, and often negotiates cross-cultural references through abstract means. Recent exhibitions include *Proposition for a Banner March and a Black Cube Hot Air Balloon*, *Shifting Geometries* and *The Other's Other*, all 2012.

Informed by his Arabic heritage and interest in architecture, Ishak's works are often characterised by a wide range of references, finely detailed graphic imagery and abstracted forms. His works in *Melbourne Now*, from an ongoing body of work titled *Half a proposition for a banner march and a black cube hot air balloon*, take graphic depictions of interior spaces at the National Gallery of Victoria as their starting point. In these small paintings a black cube, resting or in transit, permeates each interior, strategically blocking the light source, abstracting the vantage point of the viewer. In the broadest sense, Ishak's latest work references Kazimir Malevich's Suprematist painting *Black square*, 1915, Mecca's Kaaba and ideas relating to institutional spaces. **MP**

Raafat Ishak
Half a proposition for a banner march and a black cube hot air balloon No 1
2013

163

SUSAN JACOBS

NGVI, Ground Floor, Gallery 30

Susan Jacobs trained in drawing, but her practice extends beyond paper to include sculpture, site-responsive installation and video. Jacobs uses pre-existing architectural structures and resources (both natural and man-made) that lay bare a transformative potential. Conceived through processes of trial and error and research, Jacobs's work investigates the changes that occur within various media she explores during her art-making process.

In her most recent project, Jacobs fabricates a rudimentary version of the material Hemacite (also known as Bois Durci) – made from the blood of slaughtered animals and wood flour – which originated in the late nineteenth century and was moulded with hydraulic pressure and heat to form everyday objects, such as handles, buttons and small domestic and decorative items. The attempt to re-create this outmoded material highlights philosophical, economic and ethical implications of manufacturing and considers how elemental materials are reconstituted. *Wood flour for pig iron (vessel for mixing metaphors)*, 2013, included in *Melbourne Now*, explores properties, physical forces and processes disparately linked across various periods of history. **GJ**

Susan Jacobs
Wood flour for pig iron (vessel for mixing metaphors) 2013
(detail)

HELEN JOHNSON

NGVA, Level 2, Gallery 11C

Helen Johnson's practice engages with painting – both its process and the discourse around it – to raise questions around authenticity and representation. For Johnson, painting is a device which is able to consolidate personal and official histories, an approach that mirrors the slippage between figurative and abstract imagery that the artist employs. Interested in the political and historical narratives that inform cultural identity, Johnson's art questions our ability to accurately represent the past, not only through language, but also through visual methodologies such as painting. As the artist explains:

> Painting is interesting to me as a vehicle for cultural reflection: because it is loaded, neurotic, problematised, a market force, scattered, essentialised and recomplexified, able to operate simultaneously within and beyond itself, able to be beautiful and horrible at the same time.

The prophetic nymphs, 2013, re-examines colonial settlement through the detached lens of a contemporary subject. Columns of current legal definitions for property rights are inscribed across the canvas, juxtaposed with an enquiring figure in the foreground. The work proposes that a perpetual state of denial lies at the heart of the colonising power. **GJ**

Helen Johnson
The prophetic nymphs 2013

167

JESS JOHNSON

Jess Johnson was born in Tauranga, New Zealand, in 1979 and moved to Melbourne in 2002. She exhibits regularly in Australia and abroad. In 2008 Johnson co-founded Melbourne's Hell Gallery, which was represented in *No Soul for Sale: A Festival of Independents* at the Tate Modern, London, in 2010. In 2013 Johnson has undertaken residencies in Tokyo and at Gertrude Contemporary, Melbourne.

Johnson creates fantastic worlds in images that combine densely layered patterns, objects and figures within architectural settings. Cryptic words and phrases are part of her unique and idiosyncratic iconography. The artist's drawing and installation practice is inspired by science fiction, mythological cosmology and comic books, and reflects a diverse interest in art, ranging from illuminated manuscripts to folk art traditions such as quilt making. Her contribution to *Melbourne Now* includes ten new drawings that depict the imagined formation of a future civilisation. These are displayed within a constructed environment featuring a raised podium, painted walls and patterned floor which, together with the drawings, offers an immersive experience. PK

Jess Johnson
We want to live 2013

Supported by The John McCaughey Memorial Prize Trust

169

DAVID JOLLY

David Jolly is recognised as an artist who chronicles the world around him. Jolly's distinctive technique of painting from photographs and video recordings on the reverse side of glass panels engages our memories and challenges our understanding of his chosen subjects. Importantly, there is a dramatic contrast between the seemingly disposable snapshot nature of the original images, captured by Jolly while exploring a place, and the labour-intensive and extremely precise painting method deployed when he returns to the studio. The resulting works of art provide a strikingly beautiful and poetic narrative of the places that are significant to him while also reflecting on the relationship between painting and screen culture.

For *Melbourne Now*, Jolly has drawn upon a store of images collected around the city in which he was born and trained as an artist. In these new paintings Jolly presents an acidic awareness of the often murky heritage lying beneath Melbourne's continually refreshed surfaces. Here the interplay between the lived experience of this picturesque city and its dark past is played out before us. HC

David Jolly
Southeast 2013

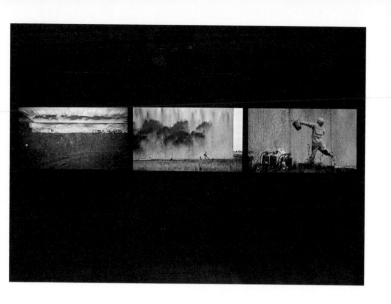

PETER KENNEDY

Peter Kennedy was the first artist in Australia to use neon light, exhibiting his earliest neon works in the 1970 exhibition *Neon Light Installations* at Gallery A in Sydney. Influential in the development of conceptual and experimental art in Australia, the Brisbane-born, now Melbourne-based artist has continued to expand his conceptual practice through film, photography, video, sound, performance, installation, architectural interventions, paintings and drawings over more than five decades.

Light rain – and everything we know about the universe (except gravity), 2013, included in *Melbourne Now*, is the largest neon light work Kennedy has ever produced. Enveloping an architectural space at NGV International, this installation combines Kennedy's response to recent developments in particle physics with elements that recall the artist's pioneering light works of the 1970s. Inspired by the 2013 discovery of the Higgs boson (an elementary particle that is central to our understanding of the nature of all matter), Kennedy presents the Standard Model Lagrangian mathematical formula – articulated here in glowing neon light – as the installation's focal point. JD

Peter Kennedy
drawing for *Light rain – and everything we know about the universe (except gravity)* 2013

Supported by NGV Foundation with funding from the Supporters of Contemporary Art

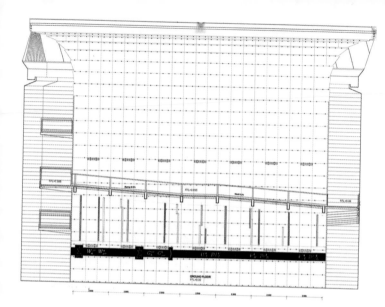

ANASTASIA KLOSE

NGVI, Level 3, Gallery 37

Anastasia Klose's drawings, performance and video works humorously contemplate the banality of everyday experience. The artist utilises a distinctly lo-fi aesthetic, one which echoes the DIY sentiment of YouTube and iMovie and authenticates her idiosyncratic displays of loneliness, public humiliation, romantic rejection and boredom. Pathos takes a particular form in Klose's imagery, in which the artist playfully lays bare her insecurities and aspirations for all to scrutinise. Each work revels in the viewer's feelings of vicarious discomfort and, on a broader level, dismantles social barriers between the public and private self.

One stop knock-off shop, 2013, combines performance and installation to critique and indulge the commercialisation of contemporary culture, not least the rise of the art market, as well as prevailing notions of the artist as celebrity. Open during museum hours for the duration of *Melbourne Now*, Klose's 'knock-off' shop will be personally staffed by the artist and sell a range of artist-edition merchandise. Recalling the defective aesthetic of pirated goods and reject shops, Klose's products aspire to our innermost (and unfashionable) desire for all things novelty and kitsch. **GJ**

Anastasia Klose
*One stop knock-off shop
(Marcel Dachump)* 2013

PAUL KNIGHT

Paul Knight was born in Sydney and grew up in country New South Wales before moving to Melbourne, where he undertook a Bachelor of Fine Art (Honours) in photography at the Victorian College of the Arts. Knight was awarded the Anne & Gordon Samstag International Visual Arts Scholarship in 2007, allowing him to undertake the Masters program at the Glasgow School of Art, from which he graduated in 2009.

Knight's recent folded photographic works extend his interest in notions of authorship, photographic agency, the relationships between observer and observed, and ideas of intimacy and love. Each scene captures a couple lying together, bodies entwined, in bed – the artist privy to an intense, personal scene of absorption. There is an evident trust between Knight and his subjects, who sleep gently, seemingly unaware of, or perhaps complicit in, his presence. The illusion is ruptured by the folding of the photographic print, which has the effect of sometimes forcing the couples closer together, other times slicing them apart. The fold intensifies the sense of intimacy and draws attention to the physical state of the photograph. **MF**

Paul Knight
Untitled 2012
National Gallery of Victoria, Melbourne

Supported by the Bowness Family Foundation

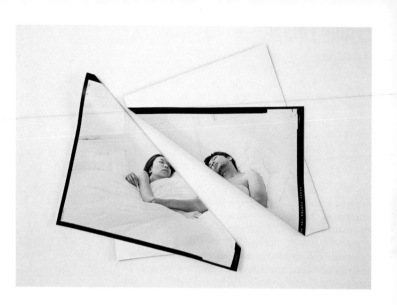

CLAIRE LAMBE

Claire Lambe was born in the United Kingdom, studied at Goldsmiths College, London, and has lived and worked in Melbourne since the 1990s. Her playful work gently critiques conventional understandings of gender and sexual normality, and seeks to unpack personal and cultural experiences of otherness via the tactile and transformative possibilities of sculpture. Manufactured materials slice, intersect and protrude from her handmade constructions, disrupting traditional notions of the sculptor's technique and in turn unleashing aggressive, abject and visceral elements of seemingly seductive objects.

For *Melbourne Now* Lambe continues her exploration of transgressive forms, drawing on rich memories of the experimental art, music and club scenes in the United Kingdom during the 1970s. These potent works use the female body to address underlying histories of violence, social discontent and sexual promiscuity. Presented as part of an ongoing project, Lambe's sculptures comprise elements both traditional (bronze, plaster and wax) and manufactured (acrylic, rose mirror and pelt), evoking a textural fusion of hippy, disco and punk aesthetics that remain unique to the time. GJ

Claire Lambe
Sisterhood 2013

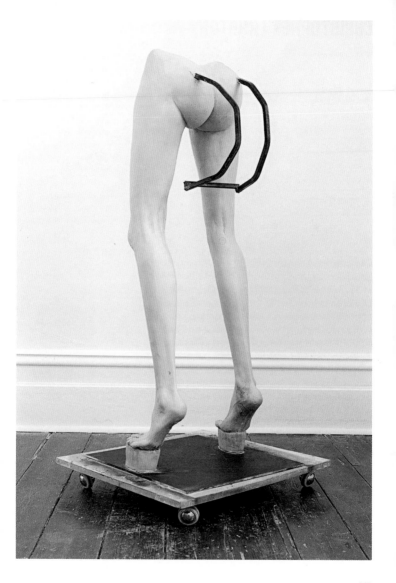

CHRISTOPHER LANGTON

Christopher Langton was born in Johannesburg, South Africa, and immigrated to Melbourne in 1973. In 1992 he completed a Graduate Diploma in Fine Art at the Victorian College of the Arts. Langton's work encompasses sculpture, installation and painting and he has exhibited widely in Australia and overseas.

As though they have stepped out of the pages of Japanese *manga* comics, Langton's sculptures are immediately arresting and deceptively playful. Like widely read *manga*, which encompass a range of genres from sci-fi thrillers to historical romance, the sculptures' shiny surfaces and vivid colours are reminiscent of children's toys, yet their size reverses the expected relationship between them and the viewer. Encountering these larger-than-life, pumped-up super beings can be an unsettling experience that reinforces our human frailty. Langton's practice negotiates the territory between pop art and kitsch to comment on our relationships to technology and consumer society. **ET**

Christopher Langton
Away with the fairies 2012

Supported by Corbett and Yueji Lyon

SAM LEACH

Sam Leach grew up in Adelaide and moved to Melbourne in 1996. He studied at RMIT University, receiving a Bachelor and then Master of Fine Art. Leach began exhibiting his meticulously painted oil paintings in 2003 and has since exhibited widely, winning a number of significant awards and prizes including both the Wynne and the Archibald prizes in 2010, a feat achieved only twice before.

In his art Leach explores a diverse range of influences, including seventeenth-century Dutch still-life and landscape painting, modernism, abstraction, science and ethics. In *Sebeok on safari*, 2012–13, humans clad in protective oversuits explore a world in which a Baroque forest and abstract, geological forms combine seamlessly to create a landscape that is both futuristic and romantic. Brightly coloured targets, a symbol repeatedly used by American pop artist Jasper Johns, hover overhead. The title references the work of philosopher Thomas Sebeok, a pioneer in biosemiotics, the study of communication through signs and symbols within the natural world. **AB**

Sam Leach
Sebeok on safari 2012–13
Gippsland Art Gallery, Sale

RICHARD LEWER

New Zealand–born Richard Lewer's research-led practice recurringly tackles themes of sport, crime and religion in an array of media, including drawing, painting, video and animation. Concerned with the dark, mundane and absurd elements of human existence, his is a unique perspective that oscillates between sincere interest, cynicism and morbid fascination. Lewer undertakes highly subjective observations of both strangers and loved ones, which he later revisits in the studio, scrawling snippets of overheard conversation onto the wall and earmarking images for future projects. Art and life are unceremoniously blurred as he recounts and distorts narratives of people's lives, both real and imagined.

Since challenging fellow artist Luke Sinclair to a boxing match at Melbourne's Northside Boxing Gym in 2001 (as a performance), Lewer has remained interested in the site, training there regularly and making art about it. For *Melbourne Now* Lewer presents an immersive re-creation of the gymnasium, featuring a large-scale charcoal wall-drawing accompanied by mirrors, sound and a sweaty boxing bag. LC

Richard Lewer
Northside Boxing Gym 2013

BRIDIE LUNNEY

Bridie Lunney develops her works intuitively and in relation to their sites of presentation, engaging with the physical conditions and architectural features of given contexts. Combining sculpture, jewellery and durational performance practices, Lunney acknowledges the body as a conduit between our emotional and psychological selves and the physical world. Performative and sculptural gestures in her works suggest psychological shifts and a reconfiguration of relationships between architectural space, objects and the body.

Acting as a stage set, Lunney's work for *Melbourne Now* is a large-scale intervention that both reflects and disrupts the architectural conditions of the white cube of the gallery. Sculptural forms lying latent with the tension of potential activation – including urban structures, interior fittings and domestic objects – are presented as hermetic objects, but at key moments are transformed into props for performance. Throughout the exhibition, performers will activate the sculptures and relocate them; then, with the absence of their bodies, the objects will become abstracted again. The performers expand the gestural possibilities of these sculptures within the National Gallery of Victoria's architecture. **LC & SM**

Bridie Lunney with
Torie Nimmervoll
Propositions 2013

LUSH

LUSH is a prolific artist who emerged in the late 1990s as an anomalous participant in Melbourne's urban art scene. His unique and often confronting practice, which includes large-scale murals, textual works, stickers, tags and, more recently, highly detailed dioramas, sits outside traditional notions of street art and defies classification within any contemporary art canon. Often perceived as simply deriding graffiti culture, LUSH in fact produces a complex mix of works that can be philosophical, powerfully reflective and conceptually brilliant. His art can, however, also be acerbic and at times is deliberately pugnacious and provocative.

Aside from his unsanctioned public works on walls, in laneways and on train panels, LUSH has exhibited in mainstream settings both locally and internationally, including in galleries in Los Angeles, New York, San Francisco and London. He has also cultivated a prodigious web presence that has attracted widespread international attention. For *Melbourne Now* LUSH has re-created a street setting, complete with shopfront and rubbish skip, that provides the basis for a dramatic installation work and meta-narrative on street art. **DH**

LUSH
Graffiti doesn't work in a gallery 2013

Supported by Sandra Powell and Andrew King

McBRIDE CHARLES RYAN

NGVI, Ground Floor, Foyer

McBride Charles Ryan (MCR) is one of Melbourne's most celebrated architecture practices whose studio-based approach to architecture seeks to expand the vocabulary of architectural expression and to engage in the articulation of complex issues, such as the representation of a city's culture and identity. The firm's *Community Hall* project for *Melbourne Now* is a flexible multi-use space that creates a bold statement of inclusivity and egalitarianism at the front door of NGV International. Drawing inspiration from the social and cultural spaces of Victorian communities, *Community Hall* takes tradition to new heights through cutting-edge architecture and dynamic programming. The space offers a hub of activity positioned at the heart of *Melbourne Now*.

MCR's design for the space is at once iconic and pragmatic. The architecture integrates a broad range of social and cultural references into one seamless arc of inclusion. Set alight with bold colours which can be seen through the famous NGV Waterwall, this stunning new structure is a space with both social and architectural meaning. **EM**

McBride Charles Ryan
Community Hall 2013

Supported by Higgins Coatings

LAITH McGREGOR

Laith McGregor grew up in Queensland and moved to Melbourne in 2002 to undertake a Bachelor of Fine Art (Honours) degree at the Victorian College of the Arts. Although his degree was in painting, McGregor rapidly established a reputation for his meticulously worked ballpoint ink portraits, in which gargantuan beards dominate. During his short professional career, McGregor has been included in key contemporary art exhibitions and has received a number of important prizes and awards, including a residency at the Australia Council's studio in Barcelona.

During this residency McGregor created a single enormous drawing, S-O-M-E-O-N-E, 2012. This intricate diaristic work, inspired by and employing the compositional structure of Pablo Picasso's *Guernica*, 1937, records McGregor's inspirations, thoughts, musings and doodlings in a stream-of-consciousness outpouring of drawing and text. In contrast, the drawings *OK* and *KO*, both 2013, which decorate the horizontal surfaces of two table-tennis tables and contain four large self-portraits portraying unease and concern, are more restrained. The hirsute beards of McGregor's earlier works have evolved into all-enveloping geometric grids, their hand-drawn asymmetry creating a subtle sense of distortion that contradicts the inherently flat surface of the tables. **AB**

Laith McGregor
Pong ping paradise 2011
installation view, West Space,
Melbourne
Private collection, United
States of America

The commission for
Melbourne Now is
supported by Loris Orthwein

KRISTIN McIVER

Kristin McIver is known for sculptural installations that utilise neon, acrylic and steel to simulate the material aesthetic of advertising and commodity production. Her work is a commentary on the rapid consumption and exchange of commodities in today's hypermarket. The artist draws on French theorist Guy Debord's notion of spectacle culture, particularly the idea that our relationships and experiences in society are mediated through imagery, and posits it within the current digital age, reflecting on the incessant documentation and surveillance of identity across social media. In her view, these networks act as a circuit of exchange between corporations and the individual, intervening with consumers' desires.

McIver's installation for *Melbourne Now* re-fashions this exchange by commanding the audience to authenticate the work of art and its subject. *Sitting piece*, 2013, can only be realised by the viewer's active engagement with its language and space. In this way, the work expands on Marcel Duchamp's ideal of the readymade, in which a utilitarian object is transformed by the institutional context into a work of art. **GJ**

Kristin McIver
Sitting piece 2013
National Gallery of Victoria, Melbourne

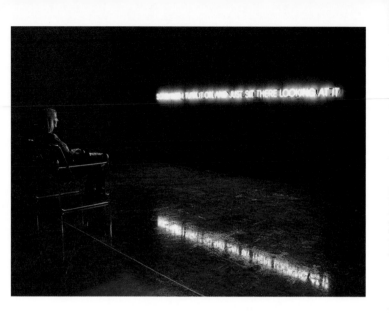

MOYA McKENNA

Moya McKenna was born in England in 1973 and came to Australia in 1975. She obtained a Diploma in Fine Art at the Institute of Technology, Sydney, before moving to Melbourne, where she completed a Bachelor of Fine Art at the Victorian College of the Arts in 1998. Since her first exhibition in 2001, McKenna has consistently investigated the place of painting in contemporary art. The genre of still life has been central to her practice – early paintings depicted a lexicon of familiar items arranged and photographed in her studio, and some of these objects have continued to appear in subsequent works.

McKenna's paintings in *Melbourne Now* were completed during and immediately following a residency in New York in 2012. In these paintings, imagery from previous works, such as cheetahs, Kusama pumpkins and bicycles, are combined with new motifs, including a large steam engine taken from Philip Glass's *Einstein on the Beach*. Painted with McKenna's characteristic gestural immediacy, these painterly explorations evoke a Depression-era America filled with shadowy relics of the industrial age. ET

Moya McKenna
Velvet 2013

ALASDAIR McLUCKIE

Born in Melbourne in 1984, Alasdair McLuckie studied painting at the Victorian College of the Arts and has exhibited widely since graduating in 2007. A strong interest in primitive art forms, ritualistic practices and the handcrafted underpins his work in a diverse range of media. His obsessively patterned biro drawings, woven glass-seed bead panels and sculptural installations have elaborated mythological themes while exploring the materiality of his chosen media and the creative process itself.

The two bodies of work McLuckie presents in *Melbourne Now* – a series of beaded panels with jazzy, abstract patterning and a cluster of three-dimensional drawings of mask-like heads, presented on plinths – reflect his recently developed interest in Pablo Picasso and early twentieth-century modernism. The principal structural element in both series is the modernist grid, which serves to anchor the permutations of form, texture and colour McLuckie pursues. The insistent planarity of his work literally takes on a new dimension in the constructed three-dimensional drawings that assume the presence of sentinel beings guarding over the artists' creations. **CL**

Alasdair McLuckie
Untitled 2013

DOUGLAS McMANUS

Douglas McManus is a textile artist with a significant history of experimental practice in the areas of digital printing and nanotechnology. Most recently he has employed laser cutting, engraving and ink technologies as a means to produce and embellish textile works. For *Melbourne Now*, McManus has created a new installation work based on his exploration of subtractive processes using laser surfacing – that is, a combination of laser cutting, engraving, perforation and thermo moulding.

Permanent extraction, 2013, uses the acanthus leaf pattern as a template to create three-dimensional organs – heart and lungs. The sculptural forms are influenced by Victorian Gothic architectural decoration and stencil art in the laneways of inner-city Melbourne. McManus has pushed this piece further by incorporating fibre optics, mono filament and malleable fluoro neon tubing. The heart and lungs on the walls are programmed to react to sound, creating a work that glows and rises and subsides as if breathing. Its title references the stages of permanent loss of chemical receptors associated with degenerative neurological conditions. **KS**

Douglas McManus
Permanent extraction 2013

LUCY McRAE

Lucy McRae was born in England and raised in Melbourne, where she trained in classical ballet and interior design. After university McRae moved to London and worked in two architectural practices on projects for retail and exhibition design. This diverse training led her to define herself as a 'body architect' and to secure a position at Philips Design, the Netherlands, in the design agency's far-future research team. Her practice continues to question the biological limits of the body and the impact science and technology could have on the ways our bodies develop. McRae has created short films, sculptures, fashion shoots, swallowable perfume, blushing dresses, electronic tattoos and music videos, and worked alongside Aesop, Nick Knight, *Vogue* and pop star Robyn, among others.

For the short film *Make your maker*, 2012, McRae collaborated with Nga (also known as Nahji) Chu, of Australian restaurants MissChu, in response to a dialogue on the inseparability of the body and food. This beautiful film also addresses issues of body manipulation, cloning, consumption, gender, science, technology and ideas of evolution and renewal. **PD**

Lucy McRae
Make your maker 2012 (still)

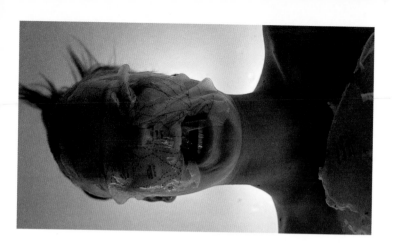

GAYLE MADDIGAN

Gayle Maddigan was born in Mildura and is a descendant of four Victorian Indigenous tribes: Dhudhuroa, Nari Nari, Wamba Wamba and Wegaia. Maddigan holds a Master of Fine Art and her multidisciplinary practice spans four decades. Her work explores cultural memory of self, clan and nation and memorialises and re-claims precious elements of Victorian Aboriginal material culture, language and ritual disrupted by colonisation.

Maddigan's work for *Melbourne Now* revisits a central preoccupation of her contemplative practice: the desecration of Aboriginal sacred sites and the genocide of Victorian tribes. The artist's intimate connections to Country and remembered rituals, seen in the markings that encode its song-lines and ancestral narratives, are darkened by brooding fields of black negative space that resonate with ineffable sadness and loss. Embodied within her eloquent conceptual drawings are animal forms that morph between different states of being, metaphorical of her sixth sense of memory lines of a distant lamentation. The work is a breathing memorial and a wailing reverence not only to history, but also to the moments in which we all stand. JR

Gayle Maddigan
Snared 2013

NICHOLAS MANGAN

Nicholas Mangan's multidisciplinary practice spans sculpture, drawing, photography, installation and the moving image. His work interrogates environmental issues and acknowledges the histories embedded in sites and matter. Mangan's video work *A world undone*, 2012, focuses, quite literally, on the epic destruction of mineral resources. The artist films a portion of red rock containing zircon crystal from the Jack Hills of Western Australia being smashed and obliterated – transforming what is considered the oldest mineral on earth to granules and then to dust.

As nondescript particles of rock, these fragments are achingly beautiful. Captured in slow motion by an HD camera, they float, shift and fall against an impossibly black background. Highlighted by white light, the material plays about a depth of field as if part of its own galaxy, the miniscule becoming significant. As part of the artist's wider practice, these specks are emblems of an immense history. Thought to be 4.4 billion years old, the zircon crystals offer insight into the earth's terrestrial surface. Their dramatic destruction stresses this geological significance, while referencing archaeology, excavation, temporality and the wider cosmos. CR

Nicholas Mangan
A world undone 2012 (still)

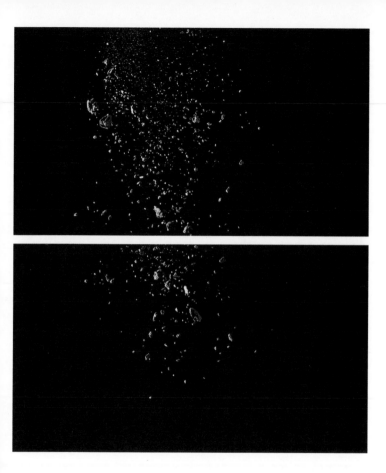

LINDA MARRINON

For the past three decades an unorthodox approach to formal and classical sculpture has informed Linda Marrinon's beguiling plaster and cast figures. A painter, sculptor and key figure in contemporary art since the 1980s, Marrinon has been the subject of a number of survey and retrospective exhibitions, as well as the monograph *Linda Marrinon: Let Her Try*, published by Thames and Hudson in 2007.

Marrinon's art lingers romantically somewhere between the past and present. Her figures engage with notions of formal classical sculpture, with references to Hellenistic and Roman periods, yet remain quietly contemporary in their poise, scale, adornments and subject matter. Each work has a sophisticated and nonchalant air of awareness, as if posing for the audience. Informed by feminism and a keen sense of humour, Marrinon's work is anti-heroic and anti-monumental. The figures featured in *Melbourne Now* range from two young siblings, *Twins with skipping rope, New York, 1973*, 2013, and a young woman, *Debutante*, 2009, to a soldier, *Patriot in uniform*, 2013, presented as a pantheon of unlikely types. **AR**

Linda Marrinon
*Twins with skipping rope,
New York, 1973* 2013

Supported by Fiona and Sidney Myer AM, the Yulgilbar Foundation and the Myer Foundation

BRIAN MARTIN

NGVA, Ground Floor, Gallery 2A

Redfern-born Brian Martin is a descendant
of the Muruwari, Bundjalung and Kamilaroi
peoples. His work focuses on Western
traditions of portraiture, landscape painting
and drawing, but its conceptual basis confirms
his cultural identity and deep affinity with
place. Martin's recent series of monumental
Methexical Countryscapes, 2011–13, created
in conjunction with his PhD research, explores
the relationship between abstraction and
representation and is constructed in a space
between the real and the non-material.

These immersive charcoal drawings are
based on Martin's photographs and real
experience of Country of deep cultural
significance to him – Wurundjeri, Paakantji,
Darug and Wiradjuri – and composed
according to a thirty-part grid that diffracts
the image. His method of drawing each panel
looking down from above makes an intimate
connection between Country, drawing (mark-
making), sensory experience and the artist
himself. The rhythm of mark-making embodies
memory, sharing the mnemonic repetition
of performative gestures characteristic of
customary Aboriginal art that conceptually
maps Country. It is the sensuous rhythm of
mark-making, which differs from panel to
panel, that maps the texture of Country as
Martin has experienced it. JR

Brian Martin
*Methexical countryscape –
Paakantji #2* 2013
National Gallery of Victoria,
Melbourne

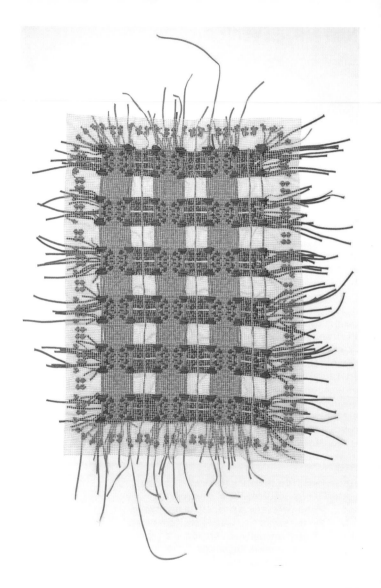

215

TONI MATICEVSKI

NGVA, Ground Floor, Foyer
NGVA, Level 3, Foyer

Toni Maticevski is an RMIT University Fashion and Textiles (Honours) graduate who has received substantial critical acclaim during the last decade for his demi-couture collections. Since establishing his own label in 1999, of which he maintains complete creative control, Maticevski has been based in Melbourne. He presents collections in Australia and overseas, and their mix of high glamour, exacting technical know-how and sleek and restrained tailoring has received international recognition. Maticevski's complex garment designs take an anatomical, sculptural approach to silhouette that balances proportion with asymmetry. His work is delicate and feminine and often evokes a sense of otherworldliness reinforced by a palette of subdued hues.

For *Melbourne Now* Maticevski has created a new three-tiered sculptural work – *Triptych in white*, 2013 – in neoprene, silk and resin, suspended in the towering stairwell at The Ian Potter Centre: NGV Australia. The work is a magnification of the fundamentals of his practice and allows the public to engage with the intimate details of his garments' construction, such as form, fabric, drape and decoration, from a number of vantage points. **KS**

Maticevski, Melbourne
(fashion house)
Toni Maticevski (designer)
Haute drape dress 2013
Bag by Doctor Cooper Studios

The commission for *Melbourne Now* is supported by Wai Tang and Kee Wong

ANNE-MARIE MAY

Since the late 1980s Anne-Marie May has exhibited around Australia and internationally, from artist-run initiatives to state institutions, including a survey exhibition at Heide Museum of Modern Art, Melbourne, in 2004. In this time, May has utilised a vast range of materials, from felt to recent bronze forms cast from paper maquettes, yet her practice is consistently concerned with investigative processes and form. What emerges across her oeuvre is a continuing exploration of colour, abstraction and space.

For her work in *Melbourne Now* May utilises acrylic, a material that is frequently used throughout the National Gallery of Victoria in a range of display devices. In *RGB (Mobile)*, 2013, May has manipulated the plastic through an accomplished process of heating and stretching that yields a range of colour harmonies. The result explores both the physical and spatial relationship between viewer, object and architecture, as well as the optic properties of the material as it dissipates and refracts light and colour. Suspended in space and larger than a single viewer, *RGB (Mobile)* asks us to contemplate what we see, and how we see it. HC

Anne-Marie May
Untitled 2013

MELBOURNE DESIGN NOW

NGVI, Ground Floor, Grollo Equiset Garden
NGVI, Level 1, Gallery 33C
NGVA, Level 2, Foyer
NGVA, Level 3, Gallery 15 and Gallery 18C

Project team
Guest curator: Simone LeAmon; exhibition design: Simone LeAmon and Edmund Carter; curator's assistants: Antonia Hardy and Suzannah Henty

Designers
Leyla Acaroglu, Ash Allen, Tate Anson, Blackmagic Design, Vaughan Bolwell, Gregory Bonasera, Christopher Boots, Brightgreen, Catalyst Design Group (Knog), Charlwood Design, CobaltNiche, Adam Cornish, Crumpler, Emma Davies, Demain International (BluCave), Design+Industry (Quickboats, Billi), Tim Fleming, David Flynn (Willow Ware Australia), Helen Kontouris, Tom Kovac, LAB DE STU (Dale Hardiman, Andre Hnatojko, Adam Lynch), Jarrod Lim, Anara Mailybayeva, Monash Vision Group and Monash Art Design and Architecture (Mark Armstrong, Kieran John, Jessica Cassar, Nicola Andrews), Outerspace Design, Marc Pascal, Anthony Raymond, Nick Rennie, Rip Curl, Kate Rohde, Ronstan, Sherrin, Sprocket, Belinda Stening (*Curve* magazine), Kate Stokes, Damien Wright

Melbourne Design Now is the first design exhibition of its kind to be shown at the National Gallery of Victoria. A presentation of localised creative intelligence in the fields of industrial, product, furniture and object design, this project comprises more than ninety design projects from forty designers, design studios and companies. *Melbourne Design Now* celebrates design's relationship to everyday life and how contemporary designers are embedding unique and serial design production with ideas, meaning and emotion to resonate with the city of Melbourne.

The breadth of design projects in this 'exhibition within the exhibition' intends to communicate to the public that the work of Melbourne designers is influencing discourses, future scenarios and markets both at home and around the world. Ranging from cinema cameras by Blackmagic Design to the Bolwell EDGE caravan, eco-design education tools by Leyla Acaroglu to Monash Vision Group's direct-to-brain bionic eye, and furniture made with ancient Australian timber by Damien Wright to biodegradable lampshades by LAB DE STU, these design projects consolidate Melbourne as one of the great design cities in the world today. **SL**

Bolwell Corporation
Vaughan Bolwell (designer)
Bolwell EDGE 2010

Supported by The Hugh D. T. Williamson Foundation

GEORGIA METAXAS

Georgia Metaxas was born in Melbourne in 1974 and began to photograph in 1996, producing her first series of portraits in 2004. These works comprised her solo exhibition *IKONA*, held that same year at the Manningham Art Gallery. Metaxas has held several one-person exhibitions since, including *Lower Your Ears*, Monash Gallery of Art, Melbourne, 2007, and *March of the Missing*, Perth Centre for Photography, 2006. She has also been included in a number of group exhibitions, most recently *FutureGen*, John Curtin Gallery, Perth, 2012, and *The Gravity of the Situation*, Monash University Faculty Gallery, Melbourne, 2011.

Metaxas's contribution to *Melbourne Now* comprises five photographs from *The Mourners* series, 2011, which was first exhibited at the Centre for Contemporary Photography, Melbourne, in 2011. These stately portraits show women who have adopted the traditional practice of wearing black, symbolising perpetual mourning, following the death of their husbands. Photographed against plain black backdrops, dressed in their widows' weeds, these women form an austere and mournful frieze. SvW

Georgia Metaxas
Untitled #28 2011

SEAN MILLER AND RAYMOND YOUNG

NGVA, Ground Floor, Gallery 1B
NGVA, Ground Floor, Gallery 3A

The innovative ceramic installations of Sean Miller and Raymond Young honour sacred designs specific to each artist, and thereby offer a portal between the past and the present. Both artists were inspired to express their cultural identity and affirm their connections to Country through cultural resources supplied by the Indigenous Arts in Prisons and Community Pilot Program.

Miller's *Fire tree*, 2013, an installation of bowls glazed with optical yellow and black Kamilaroi sacred geometry, is based on a cultural memory sparked by archival photographs of his father showing him an old tree that had been burnt, revealing carvings in its trunk within the charred wood. Young, a nephew of senior artist Ray Thomas, was given access to diagrams of Gunnai/Kurnai shields drawn by elders some thirty years ago. His reverential installation *Shielding our future*, 2013, comprises five life-sized ceramic shields bearing designs of his people's clans. In creating the work, Young felt that his ancestors directed his hands to form the shields and their geometric markings. **JR**

Sean Miller
Fire tree 2013

Raymond Young
Shielding our future
Tatungoloong,
Brayakoloong,
Krowathunkooloong,
Brabuwooloong,
Bratowoloong 2013

225

TULLY MOORE

Tully Moore is a Melbourne-based artist who paints urban and suburban scenic fragments. Moore undertakes long journeys through the inner-city landscape, drawn to various elements of design, intervention and decay, and his wanderings and subsequent paintings form a kind of incidental map of the terrain. Precise in their execution, his works often feature architecture, street signage and graffiti, with text appearing in a cacophony of meaning and banality.

The series of works in *Melbourne Now* continues Moore's investigation into the cultural connotations associated with fabrics. Presented with a wall-painting backdrop, these works take as their point of departure a fabric print, which is emulated, folds and all, in oil paint. Moore overlays this with found graffiti, fabric patches and objects to create works concerned with how we perceive ourselves through branding, patterning and design motifs, and whether these are used as a form of camouflage or to link oneself to a particular movement or status. The paintings' form references banners used throughout history, by ensign carriers to trade unions and football supporters, to communicate allegiance to others. **SM**

Tully Moore
Chevron 2013

GREG MORE

Greg More is an expert in data visualisations that connect art, design and technology. His design work has been exhibited at the Museum of Modern Art, New York, and selected for the onedotzero and Resfest international film festivals. He is the founder of OOM Creative, Melbourne, and senior lecturer at RMIT University.

More's data tapestry for *Melbourne Now*'s *ZOOM* project, developed in collaboration with sound artist Marco Cher-Gibard, re-imagines the concept of a city through a series of data visualisations, exploring ecologies, demographics and infrastructure through data. As a system it presents an unfolding and temporal projection of historic and real-time information. By connecting visual and sonic forms of data representation it illustrates the City of Melbourne – at different scales – through a series of changing data-scapes. The tapestry incorporates custom-designed software, four high-definition projections and a multichannel spatial sound installation. EM

Greg More
Data visualisations 2013

Supported by The Hugh D. T. Williamson Foundation

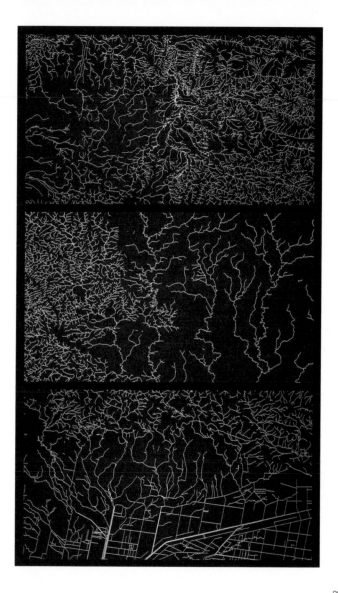

229

CALLUM MORTON

Callum Morton is one of Melbourne's foremost artists. His architectural installations and sculptures explore the emotional and social impacts of the built environment, and draw on notions of history, absence, drama and humour. Since his first solo exhibition in 1989, Morton has exhibited extensively in Australia and internationally and, in 2007, he represented Australia at the fifty-second Venice Biennale. Morton has undertaken significant public commissions, including the sculpture *Hotel*, 2008, for Melbourne's EastLink freeway, and has been the recipient of numerous grants and residencies.

For *Melbourne Now*, Morton presents *Cover up #4*, 2012, a 'covered' canvas hanging on the wall. From a distance, the sculpture reads as it appears – as a painting draped in a pastel yellow fabric. As the viewer comes closer to the work, however, the illusion becomes apparent through the decayed imprints and hard surface of the 'fabric' that dips and rises and, on the right-hand side, appears to droop. The camouflaging of objects is an ongoing aspect of Morton's practice that speaks to a broader narrative of absence, illusion and the artist's abiding interest in the effects of disturbance and removal. JC

Callum Morton
Cover up #4 2012
National Gallery of Victoria, Melbourne

ARLO MOUNTFORD

NGVA, Level 3, Gallery 20

Arlo Mountford is well known for meticulously researched digital animations that reinterpret various moments in art history. Since graduating with a Bachelor of Fine Art from the Victorian College of the Arts in 2002, the Melbourne artist has developed a unique practice based around a playful yet critical engagement with the history of art, and an interrogation of the Western canon.

In *Walking the line*, 2013, a new work made for *Melbourne Now*, Mountford brings to life various works in the collection of the National Gallery of Victoria. Calling to mind Paul Klee's famous description of drawing as 'taking a line for a walk', this dual-channel video installation follows Mountford's signature stick figures as they navigate their way through the collection. Combining elements of slapstick humour with moments of contemplation, *Walking the line* takes us on a vibrant journey through some of the Gallery's most iconic paintings – from Mark Rothko's *Untitled (Red)*, 1956, to Fred Williams's *Pilbara Series*, 1979–81 – drawing unexpected narratives, chronologies and juxtapositions along the way. JD

Arlo Mountford
Walking the line 2013 (still)

MUIR MENDES

Bruno Mendes and Amy Muir met as architecture students at RMIT University, Melbourne. At the time, Portuguese Mendes had recently presented a project in Porto and Muir had just returned from a trip to Portugal. Their conversations revolved around craftsmanship, materiality, contextual references and the nuances of the everyday. Their architectural practice, balancing traditional practice with self-funded projects initiated to test design concepts, was born in 2011. Their first project, created that year, was the self-made Law Street House, Melbourne.

For *Melbourne Now*, Muir Mendes has designed a sinuous steel display system for contemporary jewellery. The architects name their creation *Appurtenance*, and describe its elements as:

> Jewellery; an intimate scale; intimate execution; lots of love; raw material that is cut, folded, manipulated; material that is refined, worked to generate an ornamental condition; display; the space; a corridor; a thoroughfare; a delicate yet robust system that celebrates the individual; a singular gesture that unites; the linking of parts to form one.

Muir Mendes team
Amy Muir, Bruno Mendes, James Burrell, Esteban Montecinos; Steel fabrication: Ivanoff Design; Acrylic fabrication: Icreate

Muir Mendes
Appurtenance 2013 (detail)

EM

CLINTON NAIN

NGVA, Ground Floor, Gallery 3B

Melbourne-based Clinton Nain is a descendant of the Meriam Mir, Gu Gu and Ku Ku peoples. His work focuses on the ironies of being an Indigenous person living and working in inner Melbourne, as expressed through complex imagery, collage, installation and performance art. He uses bitumen, bleach and other unconventional materials as a lament for the invasion of roads, degradation of the natural environment and the whitening of Indigenous Australia.

Nain's *Chicken feed*, 2013, was inspired by the 1937 speech by Aboriginal political activist Pastor Sir Douglas Nicholls, a close friend of Nain's mother, Eleanor Harding. Nicholls's defiant words of resistance, 'We soar like eagles and they feed us like chickens', rail against the oppression, containment and unconscionable hardship of Aboriginal people at the hands of whitefella colonisers. Nain's work rages against the fact that while many Aboriginal people live below the poverty line, non-Indigenous people prosper through the mining of land that was stolen from them. His gestural painting and performance-based installation is dedicated to Sir Douglas Nicholls and Gladys Nicholls – and to all the eagles that soar. JR

Clinton Nain
Run and jump 2008
National Gallery of Victoria, Melbourne

ELIZABETH NEWMAN

Elizabeth Newman's practice, which has spanned close to three decades, incorporates painting, installation, fabric, collage, object and text-based work. Her art seeks abstraction in the form of pre-conscious and primal gestures, evoking an intrinsic subjectivity. Disinterested in present-day consumer and spectacle culture, Newman utilises everyday materials and processes, reducing each medium to its most essential form. The artist creates structures that draw attention to the lack within their own creation, reappraising traditions of Minimalist sculpture and painting.

For *Melbourne Now*, Newman presents an assemblage of paintings, fabric and text works which reflect variations of her practice. These disparate objects work in relation to one another, not because they form an installation within the gallery, but because they signify a collapse between their objective and subjective functions. As the artist explains:

> Art of this sort seems to have a relationship to time and to silence, in contrast to space and sound. A work like one of these wall pieces, or a found object for that matter, seems to stop time for a moment, to cut it in its tracks – a selection is made out of a temporal continuity.

GJ

Elizabeth Newman
Untitled 2013

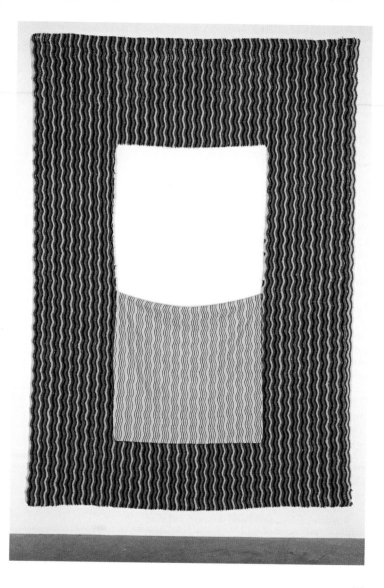

GEOFF NEWTON

NGVA, Level 3, Gallery 13A

Melbourne-based artist and curator Geoff Newton is a graduate of the Canberra School of Art. Newton's cross-disciplinary approach allows him to work in various media, including painting, collage, sound and performance, and to work collaboratively with other artists, producing a dynamic, self-reflexive and multifaceted body of work.

In *Behind the scene*, 2013, Newton refers to the art world as a site for critical dialogue, the exchange of ideas and the constant re-evaluation of history. By depicting the cover of an issue of 1980s Melbourne art magazine *Tension*, Newton reflects on shifts in contemporary practice over the past two decades. The January 1990 edition of *Tension* is a testament to how art was promoted and discussed prior to the global recession of the early 1990s (shortly before the magazine ceased publication), which Newton aligns to today's mobilised commodification of culture. With a dynamic, confusing optical style that recalls printing mis-registration, Newton muses on the role of the media and the relevance of criticism in contemporary practice, while also evoking the ways in which art history continues to haunt the present. **AR**

Geoff Newton
Work in progress (studio) 2013

PHUONG NGO

NGVA, Ground Floor, Studio B

Phuong Ngo's works of art investigate both his personal identity as the son of Vietnamese refugees, and his collective identity as a member of the twentieth-century Vietnamese diaspora. Ngo uses the moving image, photography, sound, performance and collected objects to encourage us to contemplate and relive the complex history, politics, war and culture of his heritage, as well as to understand the refugee experience that has become an integral aspect of Melbourne's diverse cultural identity.

In *Melbourne Now* Ngo displays an extensive selection of 35 mm slides from *The Vietnam Archive Project*, 2010–, in custom-built lightbox tables. The audience is invited to examine the images through viewers provided and gain a vivid and intimate experience of the subject. This personal engagement with events that profoundly changed the lives of millions and altered our perceptions of war offers a close-up view of the real-time experience from this period in Vietnamese history. The work also examines the wider legacies of colonialism, war and the global displacement of people. **WC**

Phuong Ngo
Look past 2013

Supported by Tam Vu, Vitae Partners

243

TOM NICHOLSON

Although Tom Nicholson's work most often begins with drawing, his projects encompass video, writing, spoken and choral pieces and participatory events. Nicholson also works with others, including ongoing collaborations with artist Raafat Ishak, writer Tony Birch, composer Andrew Byrne and artist, designer and publisher Brad Haylock. His work explores memorialisation, how our understanding of the past might animate our future actions and the different ways images feed this process of imagination and animation.

Comparative monument (Palestine), 2012, is a proposition for a future monument and takes the form of nine stacks of posters – which visitors may take and display where they live. The work began with searching for war monuments bearing the name 'Palestine', erected in and around Melbourne in the early 1920s to commemorate the presence of Australian troops in Palestine during the First World War. Originally pasted up around the streets of Ramallah, the posters are an attempt to reanimate these Australian imperial memorials. *Comparative monument (Palestine)* rethinks the nature and possibilities of the monument as a tradition, and suggests new forms of connection between different parts of the world and their histories. **AR & SM**

Tom Nicholson
*Comparative monument
(Palestine)* 2012
installation view, Qalandiya
International, Ramallah,
Palestine

TOMISLAV NIKOLIC

NGVI, Level 3, Gallery 38C

Melbourne-born painter Tomislav Nikolic's paintings are complex investigations of colour. His work is laden with multiple reference points – from art history to music and pop culture. In the past Nikolic has created evocative paintings that synthesise his recollections and strong emotive responses to renowned works of art. Increasingly, however, Nikolic looks to conflate these personal recollections with a more systemic investigation of colour theories.

The titles of Nikolic's works can be evocative and deeply nostalgic, yet his paintings assert their own life independently of that memory. His work in *Melbourne Now*, *3: we all have a dream of a place we belong*, 2013, for example, borrows its title from a line in the Pet Shop Boys' song 'Here'. In this work muted layers of mauve, white and pink are framed by a sharp, contrasting lime green: dramatically different tones that somehow appear harmonious in this context. Nikolic's oeuvre is a complex visual autobiography, but its breadth of reference leaves it open to interpretation. **NA**

Tomislav Nikolic
3: we all have a dream of a place we belong 2013

ROSE NOLAN

NGVA, Ground Floor, Foyer
NGVA, Level 3, Foyer

Inspired by the revolutionary aesthetics of Russian Constructivism, the sculpture and text-based practice of Rose Nolan belies a wistful longing for past moments of collective political urgency. At the same time, however, she blurs the line between grandeur and failure; her flags are anti-monumental, her large-scale constructions employ humble materials, such as cardboard and hessian, and her pamphlets and books are rough and self-published. Nolan imbues her practice with a self-deprecating humour that questions her role as an artist as well as her implication in broader social and ideological value systems.

Nolan's contribution to *Melbourne Now* is *Big Words (Not Mine) – Read the words "public space"...*, 2013, a 100-metre strip of bunting emblazoned with text from a lecture by the American performance artist Vito Acconci entitled 'Public Space in a Private Time' (1995), which fervently calls for the discursive and revolutionary potential of non-commercial public space. Situated in a prominant position at The Ian Potter Centre: NGV Australia, Nolan's piece injects a hint of festive irony into discussions surrounding democratic space, public values and institutions of art. **LC**

Rose Nolan
Big Words (Not Mine) – Read the words "public space"...
2013 (detail)

249

NOW HEAR THIS

NGVA, Level 2, Gallery 11E
NGVA, Level 3, Gallery 16D

Sound art and experimental music is an area of creative practice that in its very constitution is diverse, with any combination of musical instruments, electronic effects, sampling, location recording, vocal manipulation and computer processing and editing used for compositions, installations and performances. It is a form pursued by a wide range of artists, from lone practitioners in bedroom studios to extended collaborative groups responding to specific sites and conditions, performing everything from discrete crafted compositions to improvised, responsive and durational works that evolve organically.

Melbourne Now celebrates the city's thriving and internationally recognised sound art and experimental music scene through *Now Hear This* – a program of immersive, experiential and arresting works curated by notable practitioners. Each guest curator has selected ten pieces, including examples of their own work, around a thematic category that captures a slice of the extensive local activity in these fields. Some themes refer to technical sound art processes, others to conceptual approaches to practice. SM

Project contexts and curators
Avant-garde composition: Stéphanie Kabanyana Kanyandekwe; Disruptions: Oren Ambarchi; Electro-acoustic composition: Thembi Soddell; In-situ: Camilla Hannan and Eamon Sprod; Place: Philip Samartzis; Sound and performance: Emily Siddons; Visual art and sound: Max Delany, Maggie Finch and Simon Maidment

Robin Fox
Laser performance 2013

ON TOP OF THE WORLD: FLAGS FOR MELBOURNE

NGVI, Ground Floor, Great Hall
16 sites across the city of Melbourne

On Top of the World: Flags for Melbourne is a public art project presenting artists' flags designed to be flown from flagpoles across the City of Melbourne, and concurrently displayed in the Great Hall at NGV International. Extending *Melbourne Now* into the city at large, participating artists consider the symbolic, semantic and decorative potential of flags, commemorating and encouraging new conversations about specific sites of social, cultural, political and architectural relevance.

Flag flying, like nationalism, has progressive and regressive faces. Often aligned with the triumphant, flags also inspire the rallying of resistance movements, countercultures, community festivals, celebrations and parades. Events such as the Cronulla riots in 2005 challenge the claims of any flag to represent unity. Developed by Stewart Russell of Melbourne's Spacecraft in collaboration with the NGV and sixteen contributing artists, *On Top of the World: Flags for Melbourne* presents alternative opportunities for flag-waving, rejoicing in the ambiguous and contested poetics of symbolic community representation. In their appeal to a wide and diverse public, these flags invite us to express and debate questions of place and cultural identity, communication and belonging. **MD & SR**

Artists
Brook Andrew, Peter Atkins, Jon Campbell, Aleks Danko, Kate Daw, Destiny Deacon, Matthew Griffin, Helen Johnson, Callum Morton, Tom Nicholson, Rosslynd Piggot, S!X, Hanna Tai, Tin & Ed, John Warwicker, Annie Wu

Flags for Melbourne 2013

Supported by the City of Melbourne

SELINA OU

Selina Ou was born in Malaysia in 1977 and arrived in Melbourne in 1979. She studied photography at the Victorian College of the Arts and received a Bachelor of Fine Art (Honours) in 2001. Ou is best known for her stylised documentation of people's daily routines and existence, an ongoing photographic project now in its twelfth year that has taken her to major cities in Chile, China, Japan and the United States.

For *Melbourne Now*, Ou invites Melbourne's photographic community (professionals and amateurs alike) to join in her project of documenting the city and its people. Taking inspiration from the artist's own carefully selected portraits of men and women captured in the midst of their daily routine, members of the public are encouraged to take images that record the city's interesting, dignified and wonderful community as part of an effort to record Melbourne now. Photographs submitted via *#clickwithme* will be individually selected by Ou for inclusion in the project. **TM**

Selina Ou
Luella and Siri taking a photograph of Oliver 2013

ROBERT OWEN

NGVI, Level 3, Gallery 36

One of Australia's leading artists, known for his work across art, installation, education and urban design, Robert Owen represented Australia at the 38th Venice Biennale in 1978 and received the Emeritus Award for Lifetime Service to visual art from the Australia Council in 2002. Owen's grid paintings, geometric sculptures, installations, public commissions and work in architecture and design employ formalist abstraction to convey metaphysical concerns. The subject of survey exhibitions at Monash University Museum of Art, Melbourne, and Art Gallery of New South Wales in 1999 and 2004 respectively, Owen's sustained cross-disciplinary experimentation and diversity of conceptual influences exemplify the increasingly hybrid nature of contemporary art.

Lacuna, 2013, is an expansive, newly commissioned wall painting for Level 3 of NGV International. This intense and enveloping ultramarine blue monochrome work relates to Owen's first fundamental encounter with the colour – commonly associated with tranquillity and calmness – when visiting Giotto's fresco in the Scrovegni Chapel, Padua, Italy. *Lacuna*, in the artist's words, 'suggests a fundamental ground in the passage between spirit and matter, space and time, past and future, art and design', and creates a meditative space between art, architecture and viewers' conscious perception. **MG**

Robert Owen
*Hydra – out of the blue:
Lamp black, Cinnabar, Lapis
lazuli, Gold leaf, Bone black*
1964–76

258

SPIROS PANIGIRAKIS

Spiros Panigirakis is an artist and lecturer in the Faculty of Art Design and Architecture at Monash University, Melbourne. Through his practice, which involves drawing, writing and sculpture, he engages with groups in collaborative and curatorial capacities. Panigirakis re-envisages highly specific situations of cultural and personal significance in the form of diagrams, mappings, manuals, texts and patterns. The artist creates faithful and meticulous renderings of the underlying structures of groups and places in order to trace and describe their influence on the individual.

Garden states, 2013, presented for the first time in *Melbourne Now*, reflects on community rituals and relationships developed within the suburban Melbourne gardens inhabited by Panigirakis's parents and their peers. The installation features a cast-concrete poster rack that references, in its form and material, the provisional design – including planter boxes, pots and stakes – intended to support the growing of tomatoes and ornamentals by the community. A functional sculpture, it supports diagrammatic drawings depicting the network of people and related social structures. In representing this structural space, rather than the ecosystem itself, Panigirakis explores the aesthetic decisions that underpin everyday life. **GJ & SM**

Spiros Panigirakis
Garden states 2013

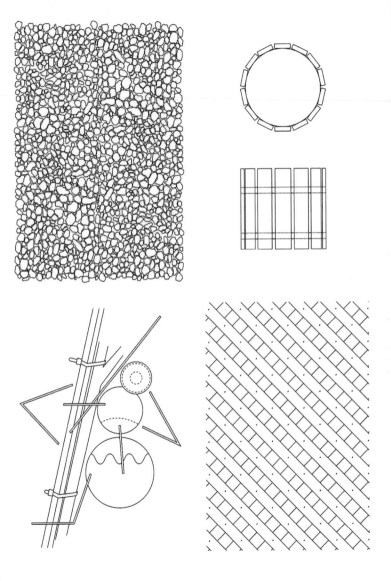

POLIXENI PAPAPETROU

NGVA, Level 3, Gallery 20

Polixeni Papapetrou was born in Melbourne in 1960 where she continues to live and work. She studied law at the University of Melbourne in the early 1980s and also began to photograph at this time. From the outset, Papapetrou has had a fascination with role-play, costumes and fantasy. This was manifest in early series depicting body builders, drag queens and Elvis impersonators. Following the birth of her children Papapetrou made a critical shift in her practice, enlisting them as her models in elaborate tableaux-style photographs.

Papapetrou's contribution to *Melbourne Now* comprises three photographs from her 2013 series *The Ghillies*. Working with her children as models and using the extreme camouflage costumes that are employed by the military, Papapetrou reflects on the passing of childhood and the moment when children separate themselves from their mothers. Young men often assume the costumes and identities of masculine stereotypes, hiding themselves, and their true identity, from plain sight in the process. SvW

Polixeni Papapetrou
Ocean man 2013
National Gallery of Victoria, Melbourne

LOUISE PARAMOR

NGVI, Ground Floor, Grollo Equiset Garden

Louise Paramor is well known for playful and poetic installations, sculptural assemblages and large-scale public art commissions made from various found objects derived from industrial and domestic sources. Since she began exhibiting in the late 1980s, however, Paramor's practice has also encompassed painting, video and large-scale collage. Described by the artist as 'geometric abstraction meets Cubist funk', her works combine formal concerns with a pop-inspired sensibility and invite contemplation of our relationships with mass consumption and the everyday detritus of the contemporary urban context.

Paramor adds a decidedly contemporary twist to her large-scale public sculptures by altering the scale and perceived use of the found objects of which they are comprised. *Noble ape*, 2013, from the artist's *Wild Card* series, extends the tradition of the readymade and the artist's exploration of the found object and its possibilities as public sculpture. Situated in the garden at NGV International, this hybrid object, consisting of a larger than life-size fibreglass gorilla and various industrial materials, suggests a whimsical arrangement that subverts its original forms. **AR**

Louise Paramor
Noble ape 2013 (in progress)

Supported by the Spotlight Charitable Foundation

STEAPHAN PATON

NGVI, Ground Floor, Gallery 24
NGVA, Ground Floor, Gallery 2A

Melbourne-based interdisciplinary artist Steaphan Paton is a descendant of the Gunai and Monaro-Ngarigo peoples. He grew up in Gippsland, Victoria, and absorbed significant elements of its oral history and customary cultural practices from his elders. Paton's practice explores tradition, race, colonial encounter and postcolonial experience informed by his worldview as an Indigenous Australian.

Cloaked combat, 2013, is a visual exploration of the material and technological conflicts between cultures, and how these differences enable one culture to assert dominance over another. Five Aboriginal bark shields, customarily used in combat to deflect spears, repel psychedelic arrows shot from a foreign weapon. Fired by an unseen intruder cloaked in contemporary European camouflage, the psychedelic arrows rupture the bark shields and their diamond designs of identity and place, violating Aboriginal nationhood and traditional culture. The jarring clash of weapons not only illustrates a material conflict between these two cultures, but also suggests a deeper struggle between old and new. In its juxtaposition of prehistoric and modern technologies, *Cloaked combat* highlights an uneven match between Indigenous and European cultures and discloses the brutality of Australia's colonisation. JR

Steaphan Paton
Cloaked combat 2013 (detail)
National Gallery of Victoria, Melbourne

MARYANN TALIA PAU

NGVA, Ground Floor, Gallery 1A

Samoan-Australian artist Maryann Talia Pau uses the language of weaving to create symbols, forms and dynamic spaces that engage with contemporary Pasifika visual culture and society. Her innovative woven forms are based on practising to be a *Matuauu* – the name in matai language (the Samoan language of chiefs) for experienced 'Super Weavers', Pau's preferred description to 'Master Weaver'.

For *Melbourne Now* Pau has made an installation of shell, feather and fibre breastplates and headpieces, which was designed specifically for a performance in collaboration with Julia Mageau Gray (director of the performance group Sunameke) at Nesian Pride Festival, Darwin, 2013. These fantastical body adornments issue from Pau's original breastplate acquired by the National Gallery of Victoria in 2010, and continue her passion for developing her weaving skills in collaboration with other contemporary artists in Australia. SB

Maryann Talia Pau
Samoana: Breastplate 2013

PERKS AND MINI / PAM

NGVI, Ground Floor, Federation Court
NGVI, Level 3, Gallery 37

Cult label Perks and Mini / PAM is representative of the vibrant independent fashion scene that has been such a force within Melbourne fashion since the 1980s. Established in 2000 by artist Misha Hollenbach and fashion design graduate Shauna Toohey, PAM began as a graphics-led label known for its subversive T-shirts, small-run ready-to-wear clothing and limited edition zines. Since then, the label has expanded to include mens- and womenswear, accessories and a publishing arm. Best described as visual pandemonium, PAM's distinct aesthetic compresses bold print designs, visual puns and idiosyncratic imagery into richly thematic seasonal collections.

For *Melbourne Now*, PAM has fashioned a multidisciplinary installation, *The HOUSE HOUSE HOUSE of PAM*, 2013, that positions its practice as an important subcultural endeavour. Presenting fashion in action, the installation celebrates the society and spectacle of the underground in its native environment – the club dance floor. Housed behind a painted facade, a hypnotic and euphoric film celebrates the tenets of colour, creativity and community that define PAM's design vernacular and community of supporters. **DW**

Perks and Mini / PAM,
Melbourne (fashion house)
Misha Hollenbach (designer)
Shauna Toohey (designer)
Black gold 2013

STIEG PERSSON

Stieg Persson was born in Melbourne in 1959 and completed a Bachelor of Fine Art at the Victorian College of the Arts in 1981, returning to complete a Master's degree in 1998. Following his first solo exhibition in 1983, he swiftly became known for his refined paintings that combine elements of abstraction, realism, romanticism and the Gothic. Throughout his career Persson has explored the often-fraught status of decoration in fine art, creating paintings in which arabesques, swirls and dynamic forms hover over solid grounds of flat colour. Yet such forms are based upon the artist's careful consideration of art history, science, poetry, music and mortality.

Persson's current body of work continues his long-running critique of middle-class taste and affectation. In these paintings, cloyingly sweet images of fluffy kittens and puppies on cartoonish clouds float behind accurate copies of graffitied tags found on walls in Melbourne's wealthy south-eastern suburbs. Painted in gold, the tags create a lush, Rococo-esque calligraphy, alluding to the fact that the supposedly rebellious graffiti of disenfranchised youths was, most likely, sprayed by local private school students. **AB**

Stieg Persson
Philosophy of individualism with goji berries 2012–13

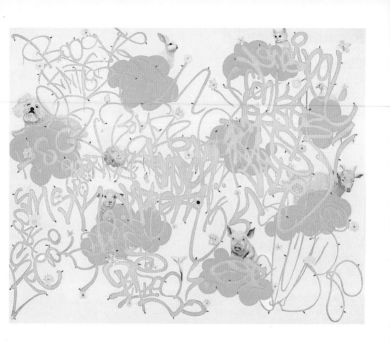

JOSHUA PETHERICK

NGVA, Level 3, Gallery 14D

Joshua Petherick was born in Adelaide in 1979 and moved to Melbourne in 1999. His sculptural assemblages, video and picture works are a reflection on the material status of images and objects in a world that has embraced the digitisation of knowledge to an unprecedented degree.

For *Melbourne Now* Petherick presents an installation of his recent *Glass Tables* works, 2013, first commissioned by the Australian Centre for Contemporary Art, Melbourne. Using his iPhone's HD video camera, Petherick records the 'unseen' glass topography of an operating office scanner (via the detritus of a dirty apartment). In these 'flatbed abstractions' the 'unseen' reappears as a complex, mystifying landscape at the intersection of human and technological life. These works inhabit, Petherick asserts, 'a realm where object and image is fractured, deliquesced and dispersed from fixed positioning and identity'. TM

Joshua Petherick
Glass tables II; Truancy cycle
2013
installation view, Australian
Centre for Contemporary Art,
Melbourne
National Gallery of Victoria,
Melbourne

Supported by the Bowness
Family Foundation

PATRICIA PICCININI

Born in Freetown, Sierra Leone, in 1965, Patricia Piccinini immigrated to Australia in 1972 and completed a Bachelor of Fine Art in painting at the Victorian College of the Arts in 1991. Piccinini combines various media, including sculpture, photography and video, to produce works that amalgamate the natural environment with simulated realities. In 2013, for instance, the artist created *The skywhale*, a giant hot-air balloon sculpture commissioned for Canberra's centenary celebrations.

Piccinini's work for *Melbourne Now* is *The carrier*, 2012, a hyper-real sculpture of a bear-like figure holding an elderly woman. With his massive, hirsute and muscular physique, the creature is almost human; there is warmth and intimacy between the mismatched couple. The figures' relationship is ambiguous. Are they mistress and servant, or simply unlikely friends, embarked on a journey together? It is nice to believe the latter, but hard to forget that humans rarely treat other animals equitably. *The carrier* investigates what we want from our creations, and wonders about unexpected emotional connections that might arise between us and them. **BR**

Patricia Piccinini
The carrier 2012

Supported by Corbett and Yueji Lyon

LOUIS PORTER

Louis Porter was born in England in 1977 and moved to Melbourne in 2001. He has exhibited widely both in Australia and internationally during the past ten years. Porter's photographic oeuvre presents a unique perspective on suburban Australia – one that could be attributed to his relatively recent exposure to these parts of the country. His work wryly contemplates our negotiations with public spaces and landscapes, often examining how we leave traces of memorable interactions in forgettable locations, whether intentionally or accidentally.

The works shown in *Melbourne Now* are from Porter's *Small Conflict Archive* series, 2013. A selection of this witty yet strangely unsettling body of work was recently collected in *Conflict Resolution* (2013), a publication published by Porter in collaboration with the Victorian Equal Opportunities and Human Rights Commission. The photographs in this project examine the nature of violence and struggle that can so easily be found in domestic and familiar settings. Porter forces us to look again at, and reconsider the symbolism of, these seemingly mundane circumstances. **NA**

Louis Porter
Signs of struggle 3 2013

PATRICK POUND

NGVI, Level 3, Gallery 35

Patrick Pound was born in New Zealand in 1962 and moved to Melbourne in 1989. He holds a Bachelor of Arts from Auckland University and a PhD from the University of Melbourne. Since the 1980s he has held numerous exhibitions, including *Bank Jobs*, Hamish McKay Gallery, Wellington, 2012, and *Cuttings – In the Forest of Images*, Centre for Contemporary Photography, Melbourne, 2008.

For *Melbourne Now* Pound has created *The gallery of air*, 2013, a contemporary *wunderkammer* of works of art and objects from across the range of the NGV collection. There are Old Master paintings depicting the effect of the wind, and everything from an exquisite painted fan to an ancient flute and photographs of a woman sighing. When taken as a group these disparate objects hold the *idea* of air. Added to works from the Gallery's collection is an intriguing array of objects and pictures from Pound's personal collection. On entering his installation, visitors will be drawn into a game of thinking and rethinking about the significance of the objects and how they might be activated by air. Some are obvious, some are obscure, but all are interesting. **SvW**

Patrick Pound
Man with tie in the wind 2013
(detail)

MARCH 1938

PRESTON ZLY DESIGN

NGVA, Level 3, Gallery 19C

After collaborating for a period of five years, shoemaker Johanna Preston and sculptor Petr Zly officially formed Preston Zly Design in 1998. Preston Zly are known for their ability to combine traditional bespoke shoemaking techniques with a comprehensive understanding of historic shoe forms. They have consolidated a signature style defined by bold colours, exaggerated forms and decorative devices such as broguing, topstitching and piping. The atelier is particularly interested in the juxtaposition of raw and natural materials and textures with a very refined and beautifully finished work.

For their *Melbourne Now* commission for kids, *Fables go Pop*, Preston Zly have devised a magical display in which they interpret and re-create four iconic shoes from fairytales and popular culture, including Cinderella's glass slippers, Puss in Boots' boots and the ruby slippers worn by Dorothy in *The Wizard of Oz*. The shoes will be presented in a theatrical pop-up style within oversized storybooks. Alongside this jewel-like display, children will be able to make their own paper shoes, inspired by a short film that brings to life the fascinating process of shoemaking. **KS**

Preston Zly Design, Melbourne
Johanna Preston (designer)
Petr Zly (designer)
Fables go Pop 2013

Supported by *Melbourne Now* Champions the Dewhurst family

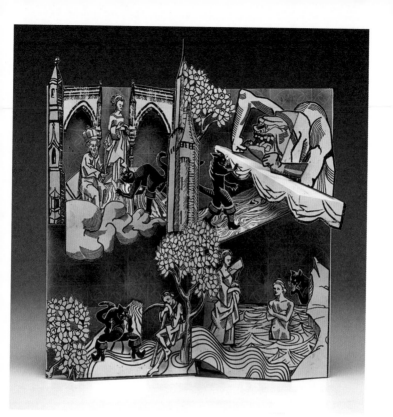

CLARE RAE

Clare Rae studied fine art at RMIT University and is currently undertaking a Master of Fine Art at Monash University. Her practice engages with photography and stop-motion animation to investigate the body and its relationship to space. Using her body as the subject, Rae creates works capturing the spatial and psychological tensions between herself and her surrounds. Central to Rae's practice is the exploration of performance and its documentation – specifically, how the camera can act in collaboration with the performer.

Recent site-specific works that are captured and displayed within the same environment have sought to address the dichotomies inherent in photography: between the stasis of fixed imagery and the changing subjectivity of representation. For *Melbourne Now* Rae has produced a series of photographic and video works. While the photographs depict her physical exploration of the National Gallery of Victoria's architectural spaces, the stop-motion animation video documents the artist performing a repetitive action that playfully explores fatigue and failure in everyday actions. **RL**

Clare Rae
Untitled (Decanted rack)
2013 (production still)

READING ROOM

In recent years there has been an especially lively context in Melbourne of independent art magazines and journals developed by a new generation of editors and writers, artists and designers. These include *Discipline*, *Higher Arc*, *un Magazine*, *Vault* and *West Space Journal*, alongside an increasing number of publications by small-press imprints, such as Surpllus, 3-ply and The Narrows, among many others. These have created the conditions for an engaged form of art discourse which, local in tenor but international in outlook and connection, is closely aligned with artists' practices and informed by a range of literary, philosophical, theoretical and art-historical positions.

This recent phenomenon also includes a growing number of blogs and online publishing projects, and builds upon the legacy of earlier decades, such as the 1980s, during which Melbourne magazines including *Agenda*, *Art & Text*, *Lip* and *Tension* convincingly shaped and articulated the conditions for a sophisticated form of art practice and discourse to prevail. The *Melbourne Now Reading Room*, designed by architectural collective SIBLING, will collect many of these activities together, alongside titles from the fields of architecture and design, at The Ian Potter Centre: NGV Australia. **MD**

Reading Room: selected publications

#78 September/October 2013 — projects Techne Architects / March Studio / Travis Walton / Studio Toogood / profile DesignOffice / Chris Hardy / Scholten & Baijings / initiative Louis Vuitton artist collaborations / discourse Russell & George / in review Faultlines / industry NADA / survey Future Retail special coverage IDEA 2013 shortlist — australiandesignreview.com

interior design review

(inside)

AR131—Present

TONKIN ZULAIKHA GREER
SO–IL
WILKINSON EYRE

Logon Architecture Ta Ta Apartments

ar

VAULT

NEW ART & CULTURE

ISSUE 4 AUGUST 2013
FRANCIS UPRITCHARD   SYDNEY CONTEMPORARY 13   JEREMY DELLER   KRAFTWERK   IAN STRANGE   PAUL LEE

Profile
Studio Lim
Hofstede Design

Process Journal

Feature
A Practice for Everyday Life

Essay
Brad Haylock

First Quarter 2013
AUD $29.00 incl. GST

Higher Arc

287

REKO RENNIE

Reko Rennie was born in Melbourne and grew up in the working-class suburb of Footscray. He received no formal artistic training, but as a teenager discovered graffiti, a powerful medium that enabled him to express his cultural identity and develop an interrogative and highly innovative art practice. Drawing inspiration from his Kamilaroi heritage, Rennie re-contextualises ancestral designs and re-claims native symbols of Australia in contemporary street and gallery settings, using spray paint, stencil, neon, sculpture, photography and moving images.

Rennie's twofold contribution to *Melbourne Now* comprises *Regalia*, 2013 – three shocking pink neon emblems of rebellion – and *Initiation*, 2013, a mural-scale, multi-panelled hoarding that subverts the negative stereotyping of Indigenous people living in contemporary Australian cities. This declarative, renegade installation work is a psychedelic farrago of street art, native flora and fauna, Kamilaroi patterns, X-ray images and text that addresses what it means to be an urban Aboriginal person. By yoking together contrary elements of graffiti, advertising, bling, street slogans and Kamilaroi diamond geometry, Rennie creates a monumental spectacle of resistance. **JR**

Reko Rennie
Regalia 2013

Supported by Esther and David Frenkiel

STEVEN RHALL

Contemporary Taungurong artist Steven Rhall grew up on Wathaurong Country and now lives and works in Footscray, Melbourne, on Boonwurrung land. Working performatively with photomedia, Rhall records an unpeopled postcolonial environment from his Kulin perspective. His undemonstrative works, in various photographic formats, disclose intangible spiritual ideas and disquieting truths present within the modern geopolitical cityscape.

Rhall's *Kulin Project*, 2012–13, is a powerful body of work made throughout scarred Countries of different peoples of the Kulin Nation, which envelops Melbourne and its surrounds. By identifying the traditional owners of quotidian places inexorably altered through colonisation – street corners, parking lots, construction sites – Rhall penetrates bitumen, brick and industrial constructions, fences and urban graffiti to uncover hidden narratives and histories. Unexpectedly for the viewer, the artist discovers echoes of Koori diamond designs in painted road signs and tennis court divisions. Rhall's beautiful and unpretentious images enable him to honour, re-claim and reconnect with sites and boundaries of the five resilient Kulin peoples. In expanses of Port Phillip Bay and a scar tree memorial, Rhall also envisages Kulin Country and culture before European intervention. **JR**

Steven Rhall
Boundary (Border Country, Footscray) 2012

STUART RINGHOLT

NGVA, Level 2, Gallery 11C

Stuart Ringholt is a leading contemporary artist who has lived and worked in Melbourne since 2002. His practice spans sculpture, video, collage, performance and workshop facilitation, and recent memorable works include *Preceded by a tour of the show by artist Stuart Ringholt, 6–8pm. (The artist will be naked. Those who wish to join the tour must also be naked. Adults Only.)*, 2012, in which the artist invited a naked audience on a tour around the Museum of Old and New Art, Hobart, and *Anger workshops*, 2008 and 2012, a participatory work in which an audience was invited to 'get honest' within a closed group therapy session.

Expanding the artist's greater naturist project, *Nudes*, 2013, is a series of collages featuring images of twentieth-century modernist art objects and nudes taken from soft porn references. In these works, Ringholt complicates the original function of the images as the spectator considers the relationship between the nude and the work of art. Interested in how images can be transformed by simple interventions, Ringholt opens possibilities for new narratives to emerge between the nude, the object and the audience. **AR**

Stuart Ringholt
Nudes 2013 (detail)

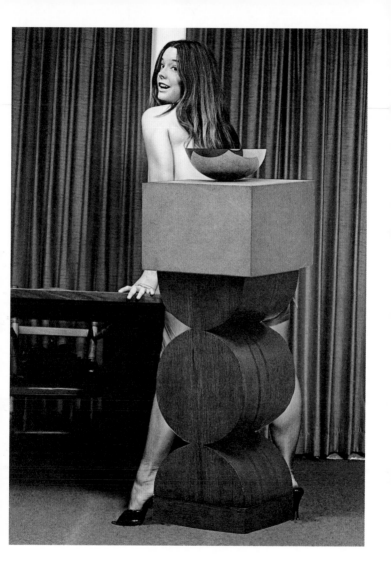

CAMERON ROBBINS

Visual and sound artist Cameron Robbins has been described as a collaborator with nature. In the tradition of land art, he creates site-specific installations that make tangible the underlying structures and rhythms of natural phenomena, such as ocean currents and wind. To harness kinetic energy, Robbins invents and constructs mechanical systems by employing his engineering skills and resourcefulness. He has produced works incorporating wind drawings and sound composition in abandoned buildings, art galleries and outdoor locations across Australia and internationally.

For *Melbourne Now,* Robbins has created *Climate control,* 2013, a kinetic drawing machine in NGV International's Grollo Equiset Garden that is powered by the wind and the sun. *Climate control* is based on the thermo-hygrograph, a clock-like device used for the preservation of works of art in art galleries and museums. This instrument continuously records both the temperature and relative humidity of the atmosphere by drawing coloured traces onto a chart. Exposed to the elements for the duration of *Melbourne Now,* Robbins's massively scaled-up version will be controlled by the climate – translating weather energy into abstract ink drawings on paper. **DR**

Cameron Robbins
Portable wind drawing machine 2013

The commission for *Melbourne Now* is supported by the Spotlight Charitable Foundation

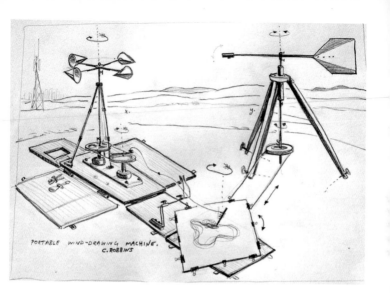

PORTABLE WIND-DRAWING MACHINE.
C. ROBBINS

DAVID ROSETZKY

NGVI, Ground Floor, Gallery 23A

Recognised as one of Australia's leading artists, David Rosetzky has earned local and international acclaim for his video- and photography-based practice. Rosetzky has exhibited at the International Centre for Photography, New York, and Hamburger Bahnhoff, Berlin, and been the subject of major exhibitions in Australia, including the career survey *True Self: David Rosetzky Selected Works*, Centre for Contemporary Photography, Melbourne, 2013, and *How to Feel*, Australian Centre for Contemporary Art, Melbourne (the ACCA Commission 2011). Technically precise and aesthetically seductive, his work explores human behaviour, identity, contemporary culture and the precarious balance between emotional intensity and wilful idealism.

The anxiety of self-expression through performance is a recurring theme in Rosetzky's work, often explored through scripted choreographies that confound genres of documentary and fiction. *Half-brother*, 2013, included in *Melbourne Now*, is one such work. Collaborating with choreographer Jo Lloyd, Rosetzky transforms a contemporary dance piece whose central focus is the medium of paper into a highly stylised interrogation of intimate male bonding and social relations. LC

David Rosetzky
Half-brother 2013 (still)

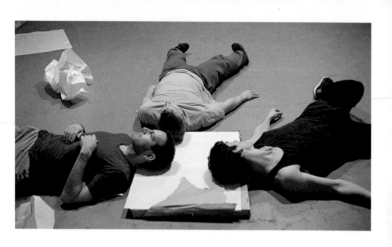

SAMPLING THE CITY: ARCHITECTURE IN MELBOURNE NOW

NGVA, Level 2, Gallery 12

Sampling the City: Architecture in Melbourne Now reveals the complex web of personalities, factions and trajectories that make up Melbourne's vibrant contemporary architectural culture. This project asks: What are the ideas and themes that inform Melbourne's design culture? Who are its agitators and protagonists? How are emerging architects driving new ways of thinking? The project is in four parts:

- A 'super graphic' introduction sampling Melbourne's contemporary architectural culture
- A projection space with architectural imagery curated to five themes: representation and the city; craftsmanship and materiality; art-engaged practice; stitching the city; and bio-futures/advanced architecture
- An incubator/studio environment providing insight into the processes of six leading Melbourne architects: Cassandra Complex, MAKE Architecture, March Studio, Muir Mendes, Studiobird and Studio Roland Snooks
- An intimate screening room with a video artwork by Matthew Sleeth

Sampling the City is curated by Fleur Watson, with exhibition design by Amy Muir and Stuart Geddes, projection and soundscape design by Keith Deverall, introductory narrative by Watson and Michael Spooner and built environment imagery by Peter Bennetts. **FW**

Incubator practices
Cassandra Complex, MAKE Architecture, March Studio, Muir Mendes, Studiobird, Studio Roland Snooks

Projection room practices
Antarctica, ARM Architecture, BKK Architects, Denton Corker Marshall, Edmond and Corrigan, Elenberg Fraser, Fender Katsalidis Architects, Jackson Clements Burrows, John Wardle Architects, Kerstin Thompson Architects, Kovac Architecture, LAB Architecture Studio, Lorell Chan, Lyons, McBride Charles Ryan, McGauran Giannini Soon Architects, Mesne, Minifie van Schaik Architects, NH Architecture, NMBW Architecture Studio, Paul Morgan Architects, Peter Elliott Architecture, Rijavec Architecture, Six Degrees Architects, Wood/Marsh Architecture

Matthew Sleeth
I don't see God up here 2010
Commissioned by Lyons, 2010
Corbett Lyon and Yueji
Lyon Collection, Lyon
Housemuseum, Melbourne

McBride Charles Ryan
The Yardmasters Building 2009

Supported by The Hugh D. T. Williamson Foundation

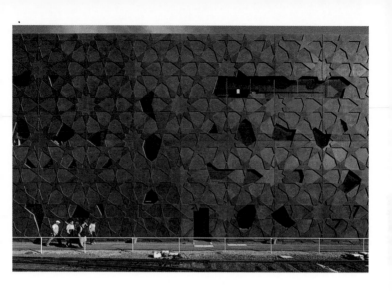

SANGEETA SANDRASEGAR

NGVI, Level 3, Gallery 38B

Sangeeta Sandrasegar was born in 1977 to Malaysian and Australian parents and lived in both countries before settling in Melbourne at ten years of age. She studied visual art and philosophy at the Victorian College of the Arts, gaining a Doctorate of Philosophy in 2004. Combining theory with artistic motifs and techniques from various cultures, Sandrasegar explores perceptions of homeland and diaspora, belonging and identity. She has said, 'My main influence remains the pleasure of text profoundly influencing how I learn about things around me. The feeling of transport and translation that literature provides is something I want to be able to produce.'

The series *You Ask Me About That Country*, 2012–13, takes its title from a poem by Faiz Ahmed Faiz about time's effects on one's memories of real and imagined experiences. Created following a return to Malaysia after twenty-five years, each suite of filigree paper cut-outs includes a self-portrait confronted by three portraits indicating different Malaysian cultural groups. Patterned with batik motifs that reflect Malaysia's legacy of migration, its colonisation and post-independence politics, these cut-outs and the shadows they cast suggest alternate identities and memories. **CC**

Sangeeta Sandrasegar
You Ask Me About That Country 2012–13 (detail)

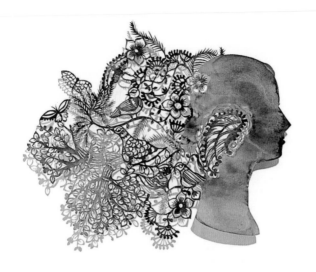

GARETH SANSOM

NGVA, Level 3, Gallery 18B

Born in Melbourne in 1939, Gareth Sansom has exhibited his distinctive expressive paintings, drawings and collages since the late 1950s, and is widely regarded as a pre-eminent figure in Melbourne's art community. In addition, Sansom has been an influential teacher as Head of Painting, and Dean of the School of Art, at the Victorian College of the Arts between 1977 and 1991. He exhibits nationally and internationally, and in recent years was awarded the John McCaughey Memorial Prize (2008) and the Dobell Prize for Drawing (2012).

In his current body of art, Sansom has moved away from the autobiographical content and use of mixed media prevalent in his earlier work. Rather, he continues his long exploration of the relationship between abstract and figurative modes, his highly coloured paintings originating from an untempered stream-of-consciousness approach. Figurative elements or text may be added later if ideas or relationships are triggered by the abstract forms. However, any perceived narrative prompted by these, or by titles given to the works, remains secondary to the formal aesthetic structure of the painting, which is paramount. **AB**

Gareth Sansom
The visit 2013

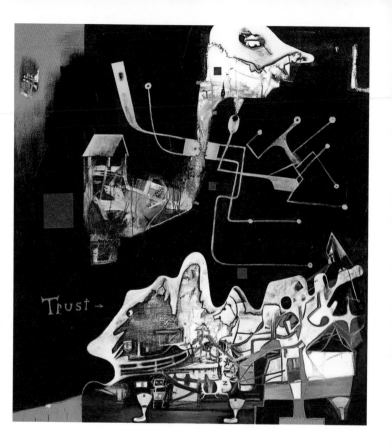

Trust →

YHONNIE SCARCE

Yhonnie Scarce was born in Woomera and majored in art and glass at the South Australian School of Art, Adelaide. Informed by research into her Kokatha/Nukunu family's experiences, Scarce's glass works engage with the wider issue of the containment of Aboriginal people, including their dispersal from Country and consequent morality. Her practice explores modes of perception used as underlying weapons of colonial power to keep Aboriginal people subservient to the hierarchy of foreign rule. She removes the glass medium from its accustomed comfort zone and exploits its potential to be emotionally and politically expressive.

Scarce's work for *Melbourne Now* memorialises a distressing mid nineteenth-century massacre that occurred in coastal South Australia, and thereby provides a place to mourn all who have died as a result of the colonial condition. *Blood on the wattle (Elliston, South Australia 1849)*, 2013, comprises a perspex-lidded coffin containing close to 400 blown black glass yams: fragile, shiny and precious organic metaphors of Aboriginal peoples subjected to disease, displacement, massacre, deprivation, drugs, alcohol, eugenics and passive genocide. The silent finality of Scarce's chilling installation underscores the amnesiac tendencies of contemporary Australian society in an uncompromising yet aesthetically beautiful form. JR

Yhonnie Scarce
Blood on the wattle (Elliston, South Australia 1849) 2013

Supported by Kerry Gardner, Andrew Myer and the Myer Foundation

NICK SELENITSCH

Melbourne-based multidisciplinary artist Nick Selenitsch employs the strategy of adapting aesthetics and motifs from games, sports and street markings to create open-ended visual systems that flirt with the rules and procedures of their source. By simultaneously embracing and subverting a desire for goal orientation in life and art, Selenitsch presents artistic situations of joyful aesthetic vibrancy in which an exact outcome is playfully evaded. He has held a number of solo shows in Melbourne and been included in the recent group shows *Inside Running*, Fremantle Arts Centre, 2013; *Onside*, Casula Powerhouse, Sydney, 2013; *Collage: The Heide Collection*, Heide Museum of Modern Art, Melbourne, 2013; and *Shifting Geometries*, Embassy of Australia, Washington, DC, United States, 2012.

Incorporating a colourfield wall covered in velcro and a series of stylised basketball hoops, Selenitsch's participatory installation for *Melbourne Now*, titled *The tactile subject*, 2013, combines references to modernist art and the aesthetics of public sporting fields and playgrounds. Selenitsch describes how in this work 'abstraction and modernity's general search into the unknown combine with the markings and motifs of sport and games to create a language of profound lyrical whimsy'. **JW**

Nick Selenitsch
Felt 2013

JAN SENBERGS

For decades Jan Senbergs's work has embodied an astute understanding of the Australian landscape. Senbergs is represented in major collections around the country and has received numerous awards for his contribution to the visual arts. Most notably, the artist has achieved this prominence and success by making works that resist popular trends and have remained consistently distinctive and individual in style.

Senbergs's significance as a contemporary artist and his understanding of the places he depicts and their meanings make his contribution to *Melbourne Now* essential. Drawing inspiration from Scottish poet Edwin Muir's collection *The labyrinth* (1949), Senbergs's *Extended Melbourne labyrinth*, 2013, takes us on a journey through the myriad streets and topography that make up our sprawling city. His characteristic graphic style and closely cropped rendering of the city's urban thoroughfares is at once enthralling and unsettling. While the artist neither overtly celebrates nor condemns his subject, there is a strong sense of Muir's 'roads that run and run and never reach an end'. **HC**

Jan Senbergs
Extended Melbourne labyrinth 2013

JAN SENBERGS: SHOW US YOUR WORLD

NGVA, Ground Floor, Gallery 1B

An interest in the built environment and its relationship to the landscape has been a characteristic element of Jan Senbergs's practice for the past fifty years. In recent times this has extended to the creation of what he terms 'picture maps', which document in visual form the conglomeration of man-made and natural elements that make up cities as diverse and far afield as Melbourne and Barcelona. Historical maps have been an important source of inspiration for Senbergs, especially early maps that incorporate drawings and symbols to describe political, cultural and religious demarcations across territory, as opposed to those that merely describe topography.

For his *Melbourne Now* kids commission, Senbergs has created a room lined with a frieze of images, including historical printed maps, contemporary Indigenous paintings and examples of his own work. In this space children and their parents are invited to draw their own picture map – depicting their street, suburb, the path they take between home and school, their city or imagined world as they see it – which will then be pinned to the wall, creating a rich pictorial vision of Melbourne and its many environs. **KG**

Jan Senbergs
Extended Melbourne labyrinth 2013 (detail)

Supported by *Melbourne Now* Champions the Dewhurst family

CALEB SHEA

NGVI, Ground Floor, Grollo Equiset Garden

Caleb Shea is a sculptor whose colourful and dynamic constructions look back to modernism through a twenty-first-century lens. Drawing inspiration from various twentieth-century reference points, yet staking out his own new sculptural territory, the artist works intuitively to construct his poetic arrangements of forms. Shea graduated with a Bachelor of Fine Art (Honours) in sculpture from RMIT University in 2009 and received a Master of Visual Arts from the Victorian College of the Arts in 2011. Recent exhibitions in Melbourne include the solo show *The Peasants are Revolting*, Heide Museum of Modern Art, 2012–13.

What are you looking at Balzac, 2013, is a new installation of works by Shea situated on the sculpture terrace in the garden at NGV International. A dynamic field of geometric sculptures constructed predominantly from steel, but also from wood and concrete, this work extends the artist's ongoing spatial investigations into colour, line and form, while engaging in playful dialogues with Roy Grounds's late 1960s architecture and modernist sculptures in the NGV collection. JD

Caleb Shea
XTY03 2012

The commission for *Melbourne Now* is supported by the Spotlight Charitable Foundation

SHOEMAKERS

This installation highlights recent work by six shoemakers who exemplify the current resurgence in traditional bespoke shoemaking practices in Melbourne. Over the last few years, a growing number of makers have begun working in small studios around Melbourne – from the Nicholas Building on Swanston Street to warehouses in Brunswick – and utilising tools, lasts and machinery retrieved from dusty, abandoned workshops. In doing so, they have revived a creative practice in decline and brought it to a new audience that values the handmade.

The shoemakers – Claire Best, Phong Chi Lai, Brendan Dwyer, Theo Hassett, Preston Zly Design and Jess Cameron-Wootten – come from a range of backgrounds and are largely self-taught or trained via old-school apprenticeship-style tutelage. Featuring both men's and women's shoes, this display situates modern interpretations of classics, such as the lace-up brogue and ankle boot, alongside innovative hybrid shoes that incorporate unexpected materials or sculptural approaches to designing footwear. The installation enables people to better appreciate the extraordinary craftsmanship involved in creating shoes from scratch, and alludes to the dynamic Melbourne-based revival of the art of shoemaking. **KS**

Shoe lasts from the studio of Preston Zly Design 2013

The project for *Melbourne Now* is supported by MECCA Cosmetica

315

SIBLING

SIBLING is a Melbourne design collective that works at the intersection of architecture, urbanism, cultural analysis and graphic communication to produce new and unexpected spatial outcomes. SIBLING's approach insists on intelligent forms developed from a positive, socially engaged agenda. The practice is a network of eight people – Amelia Borg, Nicholas Braun, Jonathan Brener, Jessica Brent, Jane Caught, Qianyi Lim, Timothy Moore and Alan Ting – who are all trained in architecture and work actively across the globe. Additional fields of expertise include landscape architecture, graphic design, cultural studies and commerce.

The reading room designed by SIBLING for *Melbourne Now* occupies an interstitial or 'in-between' space at The Ian Potter Centre: NGV Australia. This room has been created to allow a moment of pause to ingest some of the wonderful independent publishing, graphic design and writing of Melbourne's art, architecture and design communities. The room offers an insight into the broad array of local voices – ranging from independent bookshops to publishers and individuals – that are committed to the art of publishing and the power of the written word. **EM**

SIBLING
Encounterculture 2012

SLAVE PIANOS

Slave Pianos – a collaboration between artists, composers and musicians Rohan Drape, Neil Kelly, Danius Kesminas, Michael Stevenson and David Nelson – make historically grounded, research-based installations and performances utilising humour, immediacy and the conflation of 'high' and 'low' idioms to suggest connections and interrelations between the largely discrete fields of music, art and architecture.

For *Melbourne Now* Slave Pianos present *Sedulur Gamelan/Gamelan sisters*, 2013, a self-governing electromechanical 'slave' gamelan, which allows audience members to select pieces from a repertoire of compositions arranged by Slave Pianos via a wall-mounted console alongside related scores. The *Gamelan sisters* instrument features in Slave Pianos' space opera *The Lepidopters*, to be performed in Indonesia and Australia in 2014, which is based on a three-part science fiction story set in Indonesia commissioned from American writer and art critic Mark von Schlegell. A comic depicting the first two parts of *The Lepidopters*, drawn by Yogyakarta-based artist 'Iwank' Erwan Hersi Susanto – a member, with Kesminas, of the Indonesian art-rock collective Punkasila – is also presented in the *Melbourne Now Reading Room*. **SM**

Slave Pianos
Yoyok Hadiwahyono
Sedulur Gamelan/Gamelan sisters 2013 (still)

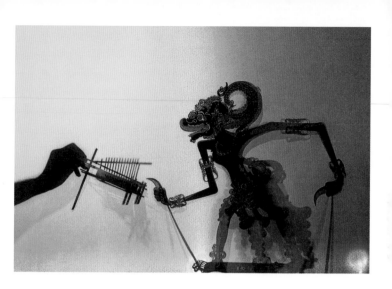

GLENN SLOGGETT

Glenn Sloggett was born in Brisbane in 1964 and moved to Melbourne in 1985 where he studied photography at RMIT University. His first solo show, *Empty*, was held at the Centre for Contemporary Photography, Melbourne, in 1999. Since then he has held a number of one-person exhibitions, including *Morbid*, Albury Regional Art Gallery, 2009, and *Cheaper and Deeper*, Australian Centre for Photography, Sydney, 2007. In 2013 Sloggett was included in the group show *We Used to Talk about Love: Balnaves Contemporary Photomedia*, at the Art Gallery of New South Wales, Sydney.

In *Melbourne Now* Sloggett shows six photographs from the series *A White Trash (Lost) Love Story*, 2009–11. Photographed in the dilapidated fringes of Australian suburbia, his images are familiar scenes of the everyday in which things are not quite right. Images such as *Plastic flowers*, 2010, in which cheaply produced bouquets of artificial flowers sit alongside a weed-infested nature strip, are as unsettling as they are familiar. However, in this photograph, as is the case with many of Sloggett's works, there is a defiant humour implicit in the way people 'make do'. SvW

Glenn Sloggett
Reservoir dog 2011

Supported by The Sunraysia Foundation

SLOW ART COLLECTIVE

Founded in 2009, Slow Art Collective (SAC) is a group of artists whose members – Tony Adams, Chaco Kato and Dylan Martorell – explore ethics relating to production and consumption, sustainability, the environment, DIY culture and creative practices through collaboration and improvisation. Focusing on the act of making, SAC's process-driven, interdisciplinary practice is positioned within the broader 'slow movement' philosophy. Reinforcing connections to people and place, SAC encourages contemplation of what we use, how we use it and the notion of expanding time.

Their *Melbourne Now* commission for kids, *MALARKY*, 2013, is a site-specific installation made from recycled materials. In the spirit of bricolage, this environmental work resembles a makeshift domestic dwelling of interconnected cave-like spaces, inhabited by a fictitious (yet absent) character. Salvaged materials are utilised to create a multipurpose space that explores domestic living – eating, sleeping, washing, entertaining and relaxing. As each viewer enters the dwelling, he or she becomes the inhabitant. **DR**

Slow Art Collective
Double happiness B&B 2012
installation view, Gertrude Contemporary, Melbourne

Supported by *Melbourne Now* Champions the Dewhurst family

KATE SMITH

Born in Cootamundra, New South Wales, in 1980, Kate Smith graduated in painting, drawing and printmaking from the Canberra School of Art and in art history from the Australian National University in 2005. Since 2006 she has lived and worked in Melbourne. Smith has undertaken several studio residencies, including at Artspace, Sydney (2011), Gertrude Contemporary, Melbourne (2010–11) and the Gippsland Centre for Art and Design (2013), and she has exhibited widely in solo and group exhibitions in Australia and New Zealand.

Smith's desire to present two-dimensional paintings with a three-dimensional quality has been central to her art in recent years. It is not only the bold colours and dynamic patterning which make her compositions shift off the surface, but also their carefully considered spatial installation that presents them as work with kinetic values. Smith continues this train of thought in recent small paintings included in *Melbourne Now*. Set against the expansive exhibition space, the subtle gestures in these canvases become part of an energetic project bringing to light the smaller delights of experimentation in painting. **AR**

Kate Smith
Orange reserve 2011–12

CHARLIE SOFO

Charlie Sofo graduated from the School of Art, Australian National University, Canberra, in 2005, held his first solo exhibition in 2006, and received his Master of Fine Art from the Victorian College of the Arts, Melbourne, in 2012. The artist utilises photography, sculpture, audio and video to create serialised catalogues of everyday findings, a precise methodology which speaks to the conceptual and anthropological underpinnings of his art. Sofo's interest lies not in the fetishisation of objects, but in their relation to specific people and events.

The video *33 objects that can fit through the hole in my pocket*, 2013, comprises a sequence of short vignettes in which the camera remains focused on the artist's feet as various objects fall down his trouser leg and are shaken out onto the floor. Selected at random from Sofo's home and studio, the objects – including a vegetable peeler, a tube of glue and a lighter – seem limited only by their size. They are almost always practical, but not necessarily desirable. The work questions notions of perceived and actual value, humorously critiquing the cultural factors that determine junk from artefact. **GJ**

Charlie Sofo
33 objects that can fit through the hole in my pocket 2013
(stills)

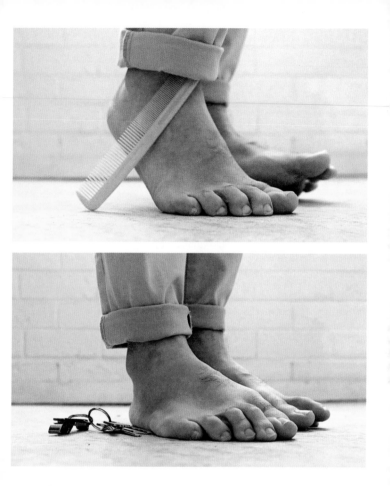

STELARC

Stelarc is a performance artist who has explored alternate anatomical architectures since the late 1960s. He studied at Caulfield Institute of Technology, Melbourne, RMIT University and the University of Melbourne, and has undertaken residencies in Europe, Japan and United States. From 2006 to 2013 Stelarc was Chair in Performance Art, School of Art, Brunel University, London, and he is currently Distinguished Research Fellow, School of Design and Art, Curtin University, Perth. In 2010 he was awarded the prestigious Prix Ars Electronica Hybrid Art Prize.

Preoccupied with the apparent obsolescence of the human body, Stelarc has performed more than twenty-five body suspensions, attached a *Third hand* to his body, and extended himself into virtual space with a *Virtual arm*. Other works include a *Stomach sculpture*; *Exoskeleton*; a six-legged walking robot; involuntary choreography of the body using electrical stimulation of his muscles; a *Prosthetic head*; an embodied conversational agent; and performances in *Second Life*. In 2006 Stelarc began surgically constructing and growing an internet-enabled ear on his arm using stem-cell technology. A photograph and casts of this work, *Ear on arm*, are featured in *Melbourne Now*. RL

Stelarc
Ear on arm 2006

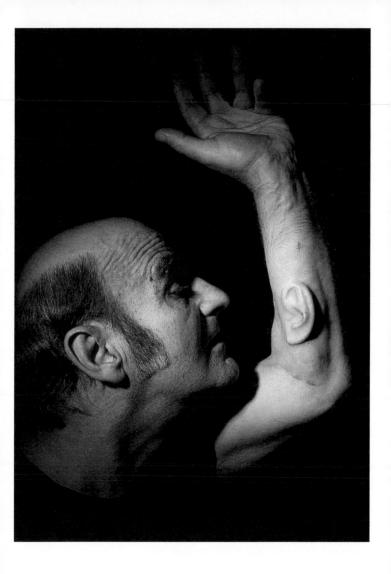

DARREN SYLVESTER

Born in Sydney, Darren Sylvester moved to Melbourne in the late 1990s where he came to prominence as a romantic photographer of the seemingly banal. In these breakthrough works, Sylvester connected the capacity of photography to capture 'moments' of life with its potential to manipulate, heighten and compose. His practice today pursues this interest across a wide range of media that serve as the basis for a reflective reappraisal of the tropes and conventions of consumer culture, advertising, pop music and cinema.

For *Melbourne Now* Sylvester presents *For you*, 2013, an illuminated dance floor utilising the current palette of colours of an international make-up brand. By tapping into commonly felt fears of embarrassment and the desire to show off in front of others, *For you* provides a gentle push onto a dance floor flush in colours already proven by market research to appear flattering on the widest cross-section of people. It is a work that plays on viewers' vanity while acting as their support. In Sylvester's own words, this work 'will make you look good whilst enjoying it. It is *for you*'. **TM**

Darren Sylvester
For you 2013

Supported by VicHealth

331

HANNA TAI

Hanna Tai was born in Adelaide in 1978 and moved to Melbourne after completing a Masters in Image and Communication, specialising in photography, at Goldsmiths College, London. Tai's multidisciplinary explorations in video, photography, drawing and sculpture present a wayward meditation on the environment around us and our facility of fitting, or not fitting, into it.

For *Melbourne Now*, Tai sharpens her attention on the photographic image and our relationship to it by placing a series of photographs on set rotation within the gallery. Part sculpture and part photograph, these three untitled works from the series *When a fish's face becomes larger over time, you can infer it is swimming towards you*, 2013, provide a jolt for a world that too easily accepts the digital image as the unquestionable stamp of meaning and experience. With these works Tai proposes that our relationship to photographs, like that with people around us, is a complex matter of legibility and obscurity, intimacy and distance, abstract depth and material thinness. TM

Hanna Tai
Untitled (Picture no. 1) 2013

The work for *Melbourne Now* is supported by the Bowness Family Foundation

THE TELEPATHY PROJECT

The Telepathy Project is an ongoing collaboration between artists Veronica Kent and Sean Peoples. Alert to the potential of the unconscious realm, Kent and Peoples have developed a practice based on the possibilities of telepathic communication and reverie. Over the past seven years their work has taken various formats, including performances, drawings, group happenings, paintings, videos and telepathically curated exhibitions.

In *Dreaming the collection*, 2013, the act of dreaming serves as a metaphor and working methodology through which alternate ways of being and communicating are explored. For this *Melbourne Now* project, The Telepathy Project uses works of art in the NGV collection as catalysts for a series of dreaming events. Seven works featuring sleeping figures form the basis for seven nights' dreams, which the artists recount through scripts and performances. Drawing on ideas derived from Democritus, the ancient Greek philosopher who hypothesised that images emanated from material objects and could enter the pores of a sleeping person to directly influence their dreams, The Telepathy Project offers alternative interpretations of works in the NGV collection fuelled by the logic of dreams. JD

The Telepathy Project
Dreaming the collection 2013

THEN POSTERS

The history of the exhibition poster, both as announcement and artefact, has cultivated a rich exchange between design and art. The art gallery explicitly links the graphic designer to the principles that underline their education and practice. Developed by guest curator Warren Taylor, Lecturer in Communication Design at Monash Art Design and Architecture (MADA), Melbourne, and founder of The Narrows, the *Then Posters* curatorial project explores the position that art, advertising and graphic design share within public space and the role of the poster beyond its commission.

In an attempt to blur disciplines, graphic designers are paired with artists to develop street posters to promote *Melbourne Now*. Participating artists and designers share an interest in print, publishing and alternate representations of practice. They are: Tony Garifalakis with Stuart Geddes, Marco Fusinato with Fabio Ongarato, Brent Harris with Jenny Grigg, Susan Jacobs with Yanni Florence, Elizabeth Newman with Warren Taylor and Peter Tyndall with Matt Hinkley. Printed offset in an edition of 500, the six collaborative posters will be distributed around Melbourne for the duration of the exhibition. **WT**

Brent Harris and
Jenny Grigg
Poster for *Melbourne Now*
2013

Melbourne Now.
NGV

November 2013 , 23 March 2014 NGV.com.au EMERGE Brent Harris - Jenny Spizzy Edition 500

DAVID THOMAS

David Thomas's paintings, photopaintings and installations are informed by the monochrome and geometric abstraction. He has held numerous exhibitions, including *Dialogue* (with Rolf Rose) and *The Porthmeor Project St Ives* in 2013, *Timelines and Colourfields: New Photopaintings and Paintings* in 2012 and *Shifting Continuities: Interventions and Microstructures* (solo and collaborative works with Christoph Dahlhausen) and *The London Projects* in 2010. Thomas is represented in major public and private collections, and he holds a PhD from RMIT University, Melbourne, where he is Professor of Fine Art.

Thomas's works in *Melbourne Now* are taken from his recent project *When Two Directions Become All Directions* from the *Painted Gently* series, 2013. In combining and juxtaposing monochrome painting with photography, these photopaintings address ideas of the real and the transitory, the spatial and the temporal. Thomas creates contemplative works that celebrate colour and feeling, challenge the perception of both photography and painting and coax the viewer to consider conceptual ideas and experiential responses. **MP**

David Thomas
*When Two Directions
Become All Directions
(Korea, green)* 2013

TRUGO—GOGO

Melbourne's PHOOEY is a progressive design practice specialising in sustainable architecture and interior design. PHOOEY's Peter Ho and Emma Young are internationally recognised for their innovative re-use and adaptation strategies that 'upcycle' and bring new life to old objects. Flatland OK is local designer Tim Fleming; his designs range from super-scale iconographic artefacts to functional objects, jewellery, comics and illustration.

In their *Melbourne Now* commission for kids, PHOOEY and Tim Fleming have created *Trugo–GoGo*, an immersive upcycled version of the Melbourne game of Trugo. Enter the custom-designed arena and sharpen your wits in this unique game of skill and ingenuity. Besides AFL, Trugo is regarded as one of few sports indigenous to Melbourne. Originally developed by Newport railway workers in the 1920s and played between train tracks the length of a 'red rattler', the game involved strong men with sledgehammers striking rubber donuts into a goal. While AFL is now a national preoccupation, Trugo revels in its underdog status as a game played only by those in the know. Get ready to swing your mallet! **EM**

PHOOEY Architects
Flatland OK Studio
Trugo–GoGo 2013

Supported by *Melbourne Now* Champions the Dewhurst family

MEREDITH TURNBULL

Meredith Turnbull studied photography and art history before completing a Bachelor of Fine Art in gold and silversmithing at RMIT University in 2005. Turnbull held her first solo exhibition in Melbourne in 2007 and since that time, in addition to writing and curating exhibitions, she has established an interdisciplinary practice that traverses the fields of sculpture, jewellery and installation, informed by the linked histories of modernism and abstraction across visual art and design.

For her *Melbourne Now* kids commission Turnbull has created an environment composed of large-scale sculptural forms, including abacus-like structures decorated in collaboration with children in a workshop prior to the exhibition, printed murals and a wall painting that surrounds a workshop activity zone. Within this dynamic space, children are invited to don an apron, sit down at the workbench and create their own wearable sculpture in response to the environment and the questions of form, scale, texture and colour it raises. Turnbull also encourages children to think about the intersections and perceptual shifts between three-dimensional sculpture and wearable jewellery. **KG**

Meredith Turnbull
Co-workers VI & VIII 2013

Supported by *Melbourne Now* Champions the Dewhurst family

PETER TYNDALL

1951– : born at Mercy Hospital, Melbourne,
The World

A forty-year mantra and a blog

the mantra

detail
A Person Looks At A Work Of Art/
someone looks at something…

LOGOS/HA HA

the blog

bLOGOS/HA HA
http://blogos-haha.blogspot.com.au/

Peter Tyndall
bLOGOS/HA HA

bLOGOS/HA HA

**DAVID JONES, ARTIST AND POET (1895-1974)
BEGINS HIS PREFACE TO THE ANATHEMATA :**

'I have made a heap of all that I could find.' (1)So wrote Nennius, or whoever composed the introductory matter to *Historia Brittonum*. He speaks of an 'inward wound' which was caused by the fear that certain things dear to him 'should be like smoke dissipated'. Further, he says, 'not trusting my own learning, which is none at all, but partly from writings and monuments of the ancient inhabitants of Britain, partly from the annals of the Romans and the chronicles of the sacred fathers, Isidore, Hieronymous, Prosper, Eusebius and from the histories of the Scots and Saxons although our enemies . . . I have lispingly put together this . . . about past transactions, that [this material] might not be trodden under foot'. (2)

(1) The actual words are *coacervavi omne quod inveni*, and occur in *Prologue 2* to the *Historia*.
(2) Quoted from the translation of *Prologue 1*. See *The Works of Gildas and Nennius*, J.A.Giles, London 1841.

Saint Vitus Cathedral, Prague, 1942 photo by Josef Sudek

22 MAY 2013

White Art Cult (1939)

La Vache Qui Rit regards the woman in the white coat who paints La Vache Qui Rit white.

detail
A Person Looks At A Work Of Art/
someone looks at something . . .

LOGOS/HA HA

BLOG ARCHIVE

July (12)

June (15)

345

UN MAGAZINE

NGVA, Level 2, Gallery 11A

un Magazine is a contemporary art magazine published in Melbourne since 2004. Generating independent and critical dialogue around art and ideas, the biannual publication is a vital part of the city's contemporary art community and a unique platform for emerging and established artists and writers. Initiated by founding editor and artist Lily Hibberd, since 2008 *un Magazine* has been published by un Projects, a not-for-profit collective of artists, writers and editors that appoints a new editorial team each year.

For *Melbourne Now*, *un Magazine* presents *un Retrospective* – a selective history of artists, writers and art practice in Melbourne since 2004, as featured in the back catalogue of the magazine. Taking inspiration and content from past issues, *un Retrospective* assembles recent local works of art alongside correlating text – whether original essay, review or interview – from the pages of *un Magazine*, highlighting the relationships between criticism and practice, writers and artists, that have been fostered in the publication. *un Retrospective* celebrates ten years of *un Magazine* and contemporary art in Melbourne while providing a point of historical context within the newness of *Melbourne Now*. **PM**

un Magazine

URBAN COMMONS

NGVI, Ground Floor, Grollo Equiset Garden

Urban Commons is a cross-disciplinary Melbourne design studio committed to reviving the spirit of the commons – areas of public land used by the community for recreation – in urban spaces. Their work focuses on people by celebrating the many ways we co-inhabit our urban spaces. The studio's creative approach integrates landscape, product and communications design to create inspiring solutions that facilitate shared experience and conviviality.

Urban Commons foodscape is a colourful, interactive and educational installation that explores the contemporary relationship between food systems and urban spaces. Located within NGV International's sculpture garden, it integrates high-tech product design with aspects of traditional fabrication techniques to construct a dynamic and productive landscape. The garden explores novel ways to grow and eat food, and recycle food waste. Visitors get to taste, smell and learn about edible weeds, wander through the 'wayward' native food forest, hear stories about food and culture and participate in growing a productive garden. It is our hope that visitors leave feeling inspired to start transforming their urban environments into creative and edible landscapes. **EM**

Project team
Product, exhibition and exhibition
and landscape design:
Justin Hutchinson and
Shawn Ashkanasy / Urban
Commons; Horticulture
design: Alistair Kirkpatrick;
Programs assistants: Linda
Cheng and Bonnie Grant

**Urban Commons,
Melbourne**
Shawn Ashkanasy
Justin Hutchinson
*Urban Commons kitchen
garden* 2013

Supported by the Spotlight
Charitable Foundation

MICHELLE USSHER

Michelle Ussher was born in 1975 in New South Wales and currently lives and works in London. She completed a Bachelor of Fine Art (Painting) at RMIT University in 1999, followed by a Bachelor of Fine Art (Drawing) at the Victorian College of the Arts in 2002. Ussher's paintings, drawings and sculptural works reflect her ongoing interest in Neo-Symbolism and Surrealism. Her mysterious forms and figures are charged with a sense of ethereality and otherworldliness, hinting at imagined narratives and dreamlike scenarios.

Poised precariously on a tripod of stilt-like legs, *Amaurots mirror*, 2012, is a recent porcelain sculpture that extends Ussher's interest in psychological interiority and the uncanny. Its biomorphic head with multiple faces, hollow eyes and swollen, protruding lips makes for a confounding form that invites various possible interpretations. As Ussher writes:

> I'm attracted to the intangible, to the possibility of multiple ideas existing together that are open in their curiosity, rather than offering a closed definition ... my work exploits the pleasure of fictional narratives and the indulgent enjoyment of serendipity.

JD

Michelle Ussher
Amaurots mirror 2012
National Gallery of Victoria,
Melbourne

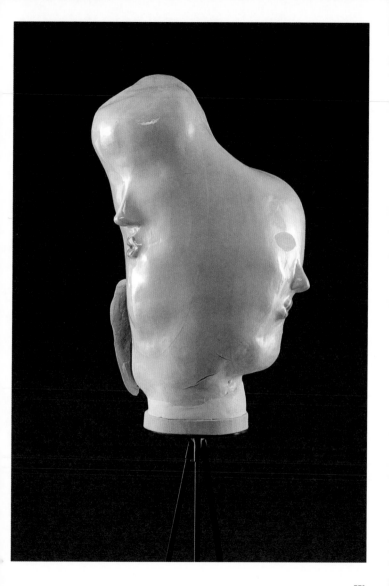

RONNIE VAN HOUT

Ronnie van Hout was born in Christchurch, New Zealand, in 1962 and moved to Melbourne in 1999. Working in a wide range of media, including sculpture, installation, photography and film, van Hout is renowned for works that often take the self as their subject and feature images of the artist portrayed in various guises.

All said all done, 2013, is an installation that invites the viewer to explore the year 1978 as seen through the eyes of the artist. As van Hout states:

> Nineteen seventy-eight was the year I started 'going out' with art. It was the year I disappeared from the world, and became visible to myself. I slipped behind a curtain, walked through an invisible door and reappeared in an alternate universe transformed ... Through the use of sculpture, painting and video *All said all done* allowed me the space to think about that moment in my life when I understood art. Being with art was an ersatz relationship you could have at a time when relationships with 'real' people were so difficult to achieve.

JD

Ronnie van Hout
All said all done 2013 (detail)

Supported by Michael and Janet Buxton

LEON VAN SCHAIK

Leon van Schaik AO is Innovation Professor of Architecture at RMIT University, Melbourne. With research interests focusing on spatial thinking, the poetics of architecture, urban design and the processes involved in procuring innovative architecture, Professor van Schaik has been responsible for promoting a dynamic culture of architectural innovation through practice-based research. Equally significant has been his leadership in the procurement of exemplary architecture through his role at RMIT, resulting in some of Melbourne's most significant contemporary buildings which have had a profound impact on architectural discourse and practice in the city over the past two decades.

From his studies in London in the late 1960s – alongside luminary figures including Richard Hamilton, Peter Cook and the Archigram group – van Schaik has developed a distinctive type of visual thinking in the form of subjective ideogrammatic drawings, which not only document key protagonists and ideas in architectural practice, but also serve as critical philosophical propositions and graphic works in their own right. Psychogeographic in exploration, and encyclopaedic in scope, van Schaik's ideograms are compelling portraits of an architectural culture which theatrically stage the world of architectural ideas. MD

Leon van Schaik
Utilitarianism vs. Chartism
09 June 2002–02 August 2013
2013

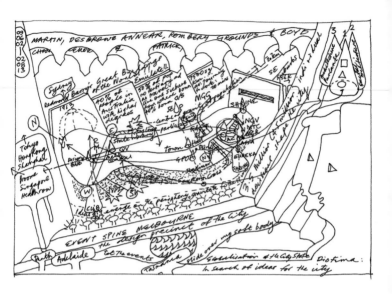

EVENT SPINE MELBOURNE
the design precinct of the city
let the events ... slide over my soft body

Globalisation of the City State

Diotima:
In search of ideas for the city

PRUE VENABLES

With her work focusing on the quiet beauty of the functional vessel, Prue Venables has become one of Australia's leading ceramic artists. Venables was born in England but grew up in Melbourne, where she undertook her first degree in science. In 1977 she moved back to England, where she studied ceramics at Harrow College of Art, London, which set her on a lifelong path of working with porcelain. In 1989 Venables returned to Melbourne and has continued to teach and exhibit both nationally and internationally. Her work celebrates the simplicity and essential stillness of domestic vessels.

For much of her career Venables has worked with Limoges porcelain. More recently, however, she has been exploring the use of porcelain from the famous potteries of Jingdezhen, China. The properties of this clay, honed over centuries of use, combined with the application of industrial manufacturing techniques, have allowed Venables to produce new interpretations of her signature forms. Subtle shifts in proportion are apparent and handles further refined to elicit delicacy and elegance. The deceptive simplicity of these forms defies the challenge of their making. **AD**

Prue Venables
Celedon vessel and white sieve 2012
Art Gallery of South Australia, Adelaide

DANIEL VON STURMER

NGVA, Level 3, Gallery 15

Born in Auckland, New Zealand, and living and working in Melbourne since 1994, Daniel von Sturmer creates spatial interventions that propose video as a sculptural component within larger, architectural frameworks. His works call into question our awareness of pictorial and real space and examine the common disconnect between expectation and perception. As the artist notes, 'I am interested in the apprehension of pictorial space and how ordinary experience can encompass paradoxes of confounding logic'.

Von Sturmer's *Melbourne Now* commission for kids, *Paradox park*, 2013, comprises a large tilted platform upon which tubes of coloured liquid meander through space, taking the form of a kinetic drawing. Two small circular apertures allow for a child (or adventurous adult) to push their head through the sculptural plane to view these animated activities, which also appear as live video feeds below the surface, in an immersive installation which encourages perceptual curiosity and wonder. **AR & GJ**

Daniel von Sturmer
small world 2012 (detail)

The commission for *Melbourne Now* is supported by *Melbourne Now* Champions the Dewhurst family

DAVID WADELTON

Melbourne painter, photographer and erstwhile experimental musician David Wadelton studied art at the Preston Institute of Technology (present-day RMIT University) in the 1970s. While renowned as a painter of canvases which montage imagery from the non-art world – fashion models, neon signwriting, advertising logos and real estate graphics – since his student days Wadelton has also systematically photo-documented inner-city Melbourne. He has posted hundreds of black-and-white shots online under the username 'Northcote Hysterical Society', and in 2011 a selection of these was first exhibited.

For *Melbourne Now*, Wadelton contributes a series of recent photographs of suburban milk bars selected from his vast personal cache. Whereas these shots of corner-store facades – windows jammed with ice-cream, soft drink and newspaper logos, handpainted typography and scrawled graffiti – echo the Pop paintings that made his name, insofar as they combine ready-made commercial symbols on the same flat, pictorial plane, the photographs' grey-scale palette and documentary presentation differ from the futuristic aesthetic of Wadelton's canvases. While the paintings delight in global commercial imagery, *Milk Bars of Melbourne*, 2010–13, shows a local culture in terminal decline. MG

David Wadelton
Milk Bar, Jenkens Avenue Frankston North 2012

JAKE WALKER

Jake Walker was born in New Zealand and moved to Australia in 2000. His practice is inextricably linked to the natural and cultural landscapes of New Zealand. Walker admits that as a child he 'didn't really know there were too many other kinds of painting' aside from landscapes. His approach to the genre is sometimes figurative, always improvised and increasingly abstracted.

Walker constantly returns and adds to older works on palettes and boards when creating his gestural landscapes. Chance and instinct are key to his working practice. Sometimes this results in works of 'weightlessness of accident and incident', such as *Bench top painting*, 2011–12, other times in works of tension and struggle, such as *Black painting 1*, 2011–13, the result of a two-year struggle with abstraction. Walker's experimental process has recently extended to stoneware, with his boards framed by white tubular, chimney-like forms referencing the work of New Zealand architect Ian Athfield. Works such as *Athfield framed ceramic 4*, 2013, included in *Melbourne Now*, create a form of wall-based sculpture further exploring the expectations and dimensions of modernist painting. EB

Jake Walker
Athfield framed ceramic 4
2013

LISA WAUP

NGVA, Ground Floor, Gallery 1B

Melbourne-born Lisa Waup was separated from her Indigenous family at a young age, and has slowly reconnected with her Torres Strait Islander and Gunditjmara heritage. Waup received a Bachelor of Arts from RMIT University and lived for several years in Papua New Guinea, where she taught photography and printmaking at the University of Papua New Guinea, Port Moresby, and developed an affinity with Melanesian art and culture. Waup recently joined Baluk Arts, an Aboriginal-owned art centre in Mornington, where she has gained a strong sense of community from working closely with other Victorian Aboriginal artists similarly disconnected from their culture.

The artist's layered interdisciplinary practice stitches together fragments of her personal history. *Cultural nesting*, 2013, is a group of five baskets composed of different types of emu feathers and locally found materials, and is Waup's first work in this medium. She is drawn to feathers as tangible signifiers of culture and place, and uses them to create objects that re-claim unknown remnants of her family history and enable her to reconnect with Country and forms of customary culture. JR

Lisa Waup
Cultural nesting 2013 (detail)
National Gallery of Victoria, Melbourne

365

LYDIA WEGNER

Lydia Wegner graduated with a Bachelor of Fine Art (Honours) from the Victorian College of the Arts in 2011. Wegner's largely analogue-based practice explores the constructed image and photographic still life. Her works are an investigation of pure abstraction, whereby quotidian, everyday objects – often sourced from her studio – are manipulated and distorted to the point of complete ambiguity. Adept experimentation with lighting and reflection has resulted in flattened, abstruse forms and striated colours that eerily hover between suspension, flotation and compression.

Featured in *Melbourne Now* is a selection of works from Wegner's *Folded Colour* series, 2013: *Full pink*, *Yellow sparkle* and *Tab red*. The careful, quietly considered placement and positioning of the objects in these works render them as far removed from their origins as possible, eliciting a sense of bewilderment and curiosity in the viewer. None of these works gives away its history or any indication of processes prior to presentation – the objects photographed exist only in these arrangements, forever, more permanent and valuable than they were originally. **NA**

Lydia Wegner
Yellow sparkle 2013
National Gallery of Victoria, Melbourne

Supported by the Bowness Family Foundation

BRADD WESTMORELAND

Bradd Westmoreland's works are celebrations of composition, form, line, colour and the act of painting itself. Since graduating from the Victorian College of the Arts, Melbourne, in 1995, the artist has developed a distinct visual language and an intuitive approach to image-making. In his imagined landscapes, bright figures and objects effortlessly coalesce within light-infused painterly backgrounds.

For *Melbourne Now*, Westmoreland contributes two recent paintings. In *Landscape with grey rock*, 2011, the artist forms a visual dialogue between disparate elements – three stacked, peach-toned boxes, a leafy tree, a bare, gracefully twisted tree trunk, a small grey rock and an elongated sculptural form – all of which emerge from a rich background of cool yellows, blues and whites. In *Tree by the river*, 2013, a figure crouches in a vibrant landscape of foliage as a gloriously blue river extends up and through the picture plane. In both works Westmoreland's painted surface is delicate, yet confident; his tones simultaneously warm and cool; and his brushstrokes, although restless, are strangely calming. Unbound by narrative, Westmoreland's works are spontaneous and joyous. CR

Bradd Westmoreland
*Landscape with grey
rock* 2011

WIRED FOR MELBOURNE SOUND

EP by Batman Park played in ambient spaces at NGVA and NGVI

A major strength of Melbourne's diverse independent music scene is its relationship with the visual arts. Many musicians are also practising artists, and artists from both genres often inform and inspire one another's activities. As a precursor to *Melbourne Now*, *Wired for Melbourne Sound* saw NGV Studio transformed into a fully functioning recording studio in which a 'super group' of Melbourne musicians was formed, named Batman Park. Comprising leader Alex Badham, Pascal Babare, Jess Cornelius, Lachlan Denton, Thomas Mendelovits and Evelyn Morris, the group collaborated on writing, recording and producing an EP as well as music videos.

Accompanying this studio project was an exhibition focused on the recent history of Melbourne's independent music scene, including an installation of documentary photography by Melbourne music photographers, a salon hang of recent vinyl cover art and projections of film clips and live footage provided by record labels, musicians and artists. *Wired for Melbourne Sound* reflected the creativity of the local music scene, providing an insight into this vibrant, if lesser known, aspect of Melbourne's cultural life. **BR**

Batman Park
left to right: Alex Badham, Pascal Babare, Thomas Mendelovits, Evelyn Morris, Lachlan Denton, Jess Cornelius

EMILE ZILE

Emile Zile is an artist, filmmaker and performer who has exhibited widely in Australia and Europe. He studied media arts at RMIT University and in 2007 relocated from Melbourne to the Netherlands to pursue a Master of Fine Art at the Sandberg Institute, Amsterdam. He is currently completing a two-year studio residency at the Rijksakademie van beldeende kunsten, Amsterdam. Zile's body of work examines the effects of mediating experience through communications technology, and the human-scale resonances of collective media memory. He has worked as a solo artist in performance as well as collaboratively with musicians and dance companies.

In *Melbourne Now*, Zile is represented by his short film *Jack*, 2012, for which Melbourne artist, filmmaker and musician Philip Brophy provided the sound design and score. *Jack* follows a figure drifting through a series of spatial environments in the inner-western suburb of Footscray: from grungy high street through light-industrial zones and finally to a partially built Buddhist temple. An Indigenous professional dancer, Jack marks his presence in the outdoor spaces with murmured utterances, vocalised sound effects and mimetic postures. **RL**

Emile Zile
Jack 2012 (still)

ZOOM

NGVI, Ground Floor, Gallery 25

Melbourne is often cited as one of the world's most liveable cities, in which 4.25 million people live, work and play. This liveability is both planned and coincidental – a happy consequence of foresight, geography and good design. The ZOOM project for *Melbourne Now* asks how we might continue to create liveability that reacts to pressures emerging in the realms of population, water, energy, transport, health and urban sprawl.

Anchored around a dynamic tapestry of data by Melbourne data artist Greg More, this exhibit offers a window into the 'system of systems' that makes up the modern city, peeling back the layers to reveal a sea of information beneath us. Data ebbs and flows, creating patterns normally inaccessible to the naked eye. Set against this morphing data field, an analogue human survey asks the audience to guide the future design of Melbourne through choice and opinion. ZOOM proposes that every citizen influences the future of the city, and that the city in turn influences everyone within it. Accepting this co-dependent relationship empowers us all to imagine the city we want to create together. **EM**

Project team
Curator: Ewan McEoin / Studio Propeller; Data visualisation: Greg More / OOM Creative; Graphic design: Matthew Angel; Exhibition design: Design Office; Sound installation: Marco Cher-Gibard; Data research: Serryn Eagleson / EDG Research; Digital survey design: Policy Booth

Zoom 2013

Supported by The Hugh D. T. Williamson Foundation

CONTRIBUTORS

Nadiah Abdulrahim
Sana Balai
Edwina Brennan
Alisa Bunbury
Carol Cains
Marissa Cassin
Laura Castagnini
Jasmin Chua
Humphrey Clegg
Wayne Crothers
Max Delany
Jane Devery
Paola Di Trocchio
Amanda Dunsmore
Maggie Finch
Mark Gomes
Kirsty Grant
Antony Hamilton
Dianne Hilyear (DHi)
David Hurlston
Georgia Jones
Petra Kayser
Catherine Leahy
Simone LeAmon

Roger Leong
Ewan McEoin
Simon Maidment
Toby Miller
Phip Murray
John Nixon
Megan Patty
Yvette Pratt
Deborah Ratliff
Alicia Renew
Claire Richardson
Beckett Rozentals
Stewart Russell
Judith Ryan
Emily Siddons
Katie Sommerville
Elena Taylor
Warren Taylor
Peter Tyndall
Susan van Wyk
Fleur Watson
Danielle Whitfield
Jack Willet

ACKNOWLEDGEMENTS

Project team

Art Services: Michael Burke, Wade Bryans, Wayne Childs, Robert Cirelli, Luigi Fusinato, Toby Pola, Paul Spence, Ross Taylor, Jordan Trinham and staff

Assets and Facilities: Tony Henshaw, Ramesh Avula, Gilles Bonnet, Gerhard Brabender, Ke Chen, Simon Donica, Paul Dredge, Adam Graf, Claire Harding, Gavin Harris, Kaman Ip, Rob Joyce, Liam Kennealy, Martin Kilderry, Matthew Kirby, John Lalios, Darren Lloyd, Sylvia Lynch, Matthew Newell, Jason Price, Vicki Sifredi, Melissa Scheele, Lynda Stokes, Dylan Walters, Andrew Wasowicz, Peter Zaleski, Jeremy Zammit and staff

Cataloguing: David Belzycki, Julia Jackson, Trish Little

Commercial Operations: Caree Staples, Phillip Adams, Bradd Bamford, Toby Newell and staff

Conservation: Gervais Battour, Helen Casey, Bronwyn Cosgrove, Kate Douglas, Catherine Earley, Trude Ellingsen, MaryJo Lelyveld, Holly McGowan-Jackson, Garth McLean, Toby Miller, Pip Morrison, Solitaire Osei, Eamon O'Toole, John Payne, Suzi Shaw, Ruth Shervington, Annette Soumilas, Marika Strohschneider, David Thurrowgood, Michael Varcoe-Cocks, Dianne Whittle, Louise Wilson and staff

Corporate Partnerships: Romina Calabro, Maylise Dent, Anna Munro

Curatorial research and interns: Laura Castagnini, Georgia Jones, Kent Morris, Phip Murray, Alicia Renew, Jack Willet

Education: Gina Panebianco, Grace Di Muzio, Rebecca Hicks, Susie May, David Menzies, Margaret Stevens, Michelle Stockley, Ingrid Wood and staff

Events: Louise Woodward, Antonia Geddes, Dorothy Luk, Yunuen Perez

Exhibition Design: Mark Patullo, Ingrid Rhule, John Eccles, Katherine Horseman, Peter King, Matthew May, Jenny Yang

Exhibition Management: Nicole Monteiro, Edwina Brennan, Angela James, Charlotte King, Claire Richardson

Finance: Paul Lambrick, Jeff Nelson, Elena Nikolaeva, Peter Sullivan and staff

Foundation and Fundraising: Judy Williams, Anna Kopinski, Misha Agzarian, Humphrey Clegg, Ilsa Melchiori, Cathy Quinn, Biheng Zhang

Front of House: Annaliese Forde, Carolyn Long and staff

Governance, Policy and Planning: Alison Lee, Marissa Cassin, Sophie Cotter-Gardner, Narelle Gardner, Yan Lee

Graphic Design: Jackie Robinson, Connor Byrt, Thomas Deverall, Dirk Hiscock

Human Resources: Angela Baker and staff

Information Services: Trish Zupan, Gatis Andersons, Andrew Caruana-Smith and staff

Library: Paul Reynolds, Vicki Costa, Luke Doyle, Lisa Zito and staff

Marketing: Jane Zantuck, Antoinette Azzopardi, Lily Mora, Hilary Sadek

Media and Public Affairs: Sharon Wells, Elisabeth Alexander, Jemma Altmeier, Jessica Hedger

Members: Melissa Obeid, Emily Miller, Amanda Spann and staff

Multimedia: Jenny Walker, Shay Grantham, Julia Hay, Timothy Hofmann, Matthew Lim, Jon Luker, Ben Moran, Jess Parker, Benjamin Walbrook, Diana Ward

Photographic Services: Garry Sommerfeld, Predrag Cancar, Justine Frost, Christian Markel, Selina Ou, Narelle Wilson, Philip White

Publications: Jasmin Chua, Nadiah Abdulrahim, Mark Gomes, Jennie Moloney, Megan Patty

Public Programs: Robyn Dold, Yvette Pratt, Monique Farchione, Dianne Hilyear, Rachel Morrison, Deborah Ratliff, Caterina Sciacca, Emily Siddons and staff

Registration: Janine Bofill, Holli Chandler, Elizabeth Hewitt, Denise McCann, Holly Robbins, Charmian Watts and staff

Project Supporter
Sandra Powell and Andrew King

The following artists acknowledge the support of the Australian Government through the Australia Council, its arts funding and advisory body:
Bindi Cole
Simon Obarzanek
Darren Sylvester

Program Partners
774 ABC Melbourne
ABC Radio National
City of Melbourne
Department of Premier and Cabinet
Federation Square
La Trobe University
L'Oréal Melbourne Fashion Festival
Meetoo
Melbourne Food and Wine Festival
Office for Good Design
tiny & little
Urban Commons

Gallery and photography credits

All works are copyright the artists and are reproduced courtesy of the artists and their respective galleries unless otherwise stated. All photos have been provided by the artists or NGV Photographic Services unless otherwise stated.

A Constructed World: courtesy Roslyn Oxley9 Gallery, Sydney, and Solang Productions, Paris, Brussels; **Rick Amor:** courtesy Niagara Galleries, Melbourne; **Brook Andrew:** courtesy Tolarno Galleries, Melbourne; photo Christian Capurro; **ARM Architecture:** photo John Gollings; **Benjamin Armstrong:** courtesy Tolarno Galleries, Melbourne; photo Christian Capurro; **Janet Beckhouse:** courtesy Neon Parc, Melbourne; photo Jeremy Dillon; **Stephen Benwell:** courtesy Niagara Galleries, Melbourne; photo Paralax Photography; **Lauren Berkowitz:** courtesy Utopian Slumps, Melbourne; photo Kalli Karvelas; **Chris Bond and Drew Pettifer:** Chris Bond courtesy Nellie Castan Gallery, Melbourne, and Darren Knight Gallery, Sydney; **Stephen Bram:** courtesy Anna Schwartz Gallery, Melbourne and Sydney; photo Ross Bird; **Angela Brennan:** courtesy Niagara Galleries, Melbourne, and Roslyn Oxley9, Sydney; **Jane Brown:** courtesy Breenspace, Sydney; **Lyndell Brown, Charles Green and Jon Cattapan:** Lyndell Brown and Charles Green courtesy ARC One Gallery, Melbourne, and Heiser Gallery, Brisbane; Jon Cattapan courtesy KalimanRawlins, Melbourne, Dominik Mersch Gallery, Sydney, and Milani Gallery, Brisbane; **Trevor Turbo Brown:** courtesy Kreisler Gallery, Melbourne; photo Nick Kreisler; **Janet Burchill and Jennifer McCamley:** courtesy Neon Parc, Melbourne; **Penny Byrne:** Fehily Contemporary, Melbourne; photo Jeremy Dillon; **Jon Campbell:** courtesy KalimanRawlins, Melbourne, and

Darren Knight Gallery, Sydney; **David Chesworth and Sonia Leber:** courtesy Fehily Contemporary, Melbourne; **Boris Cipusev:** courtesy Arts Project Australia, Melbourne; **Maree Clarke:** courtesy Vivien Anderson Gallery, Melbourne; photo Simon Anderson; **Bindi Cole:** courtesy Nellie Castan Gallery, Melbourne; **Lorraine Connelly-Northey:** photo Mick Bradley; **Alan Constable:** courtesy Arts Project Australia, Melbourne; **Zoë Croggon:** courtesy Daine Singer, Melbourne; **Daniel Crooks:** courtesy Anna Schwartz Gallery, Melbourne and Sydney; **Juan Davila:** courtesy Kalli Rolfe Contemporary Art, Melbourne; photo Mark Ashkanasy; **Julia deVille:** courtesy Sophie Gannon Gallery, Melbourne; photo Terence Bogue; **Emily Floyd:** courtesy Anna Schwartz Gallery, Melbourne and Sydney; photo John Brash; **Juan Ford:** courtesy Dianne Tanzer Gallery and Projects, Melbourne; **Louise Forthun:** courtesy Block Projects, Melbourne; **Robin Fox:** photo Lasse Marhaug; **Patrick Francis:** courtesy Arts Project Australia, Melbourne; **Marco Fusinato:** courtesy Anna Schwartz Gallery, Melbourne and Sydney; photo Christian Capurrro; **Tony Garifalakis:** courtesy Hugo Michell Gallery, Adelaide; **Starlie Geikie:** courtesy Utopian Slumps, Melbourne; **Mira Gojak:** courtesy Murray White Room, Melbourne; photo Darryl Watson; **Allona Goren:** photo Jeremy Dillion; **Agatha Gothe-Snape:** courtesy The Commercial, Sydney; **Elizabeth Gower:** courtesy Sutton Gallery, Melbourne, and Milani Gallery, Brisbane; **Greatest Hits:** courtesy Tristian Koenig, Melbourne; photo Christo Crocker; **Helen Grogan, Shelley Lasica and Anne-Marie May:** photo Anna Gilby and Helen Grogan; **Michelle Hamer:** courtesy Fehily Contemporary, Melbourne; photo Marc Morel;

Brent Harris: courtesy Tolarno Galleries, Melbourne; Ponch Hawkes: courtesy Chrysalis Gallery, Melbourne; Andrew Hazewinkel: photo Marshall Collection, British School at Rome Photo Archive; Bianca Hester: Sarah Scout, Melbourne; photo Mimmo Cozzolino; Christopher LG Hill: photo Kate Meakin; Mark Hilton: Darren Knight Gallery, Sydney; photo John Brash; Matt Hinkley: KalimanRawlins, Melbourne; photo Andrew Curtis; Lou Hubbard: courtesy Sarah Scout, Melbourne; Brendan Huntley: courtesy Tolarno Galleries, Melbourne; Eliza Hutchison: courtesy Murray White Room, Melbourne; Ricardo Idagi: courtesy Vivien Anderson Gallery, Melbourne; Lucy Irvine: photo Hans Jahr; Raafat Ishak: courtesy Sutton Gallery, Melbourne; Susan Jacobs: courtesy Sarah Scout, Melbourne; Helen Johnson: courtesy Sutton Gallery, Melbourne; photo Andrew Curtis; Jess Johnson: courtesy Darren Knight Gallery, Sydney, and Utopian Slumps, Melbourne; David Jolly: courtesy Sutton Gallery, Melbourne; Ash Keating: courtesy Fehily Contemporary, Melbourne; Peter Kennedy: courtesy Milani Gallery, Brisbane; Anastasia Klose: courtesy Tolarno Galleries, Melbourne; Paul Knight: courtesy Neon Parc, Melbourne; photo Christopher Snee; Claire Lambe: courtesy Sarah Scout, Melbourne; photo Phoebe Schmidt; Christopher Langton: courtesy Tolarno Galleries, Melbourne; photo John Gollings; Sam Leach: courtesy Sullivan+Strumf, Sydney; Richard Lewer: courtesy Fehily Contemporary, Melbourne, and Hugo Michell Gallery, Beulah Park, South Australia; photo Bo Wong; Bridie Lunney with Torie Nimmervoll: photo Jake Walker; LUSH: photo Andrius Lipsys; McBride Charles Ryan Architects:

photo Peter Bennetts; Laith McGregor: courtesy KalimanRawlins, Melbourne, and Sullivan+Strumpf, Sydney; Kristin McIver: courtesy James Makin Gallery, Melbourne; photo Tim Gresham; Moya McKenna: courtesy Sarah Cottier Gallery, Sydney; Alasdair McLuckie: courtesy Murray White Room, Melbourne; Gayle Maddigan: photo Peter Hills; Nicholas Mangan: courtesy Sutton Gallery, Melbourne; Linda Marrinon: courtesy Roslyn Oxley9 Gallery, Sydney; Brian Martin: courtesy William Mora Galleries, Melbourne; Anne-Marie May: courtesy Murray White Room; photo John Brash; Georgia Metaxas: courtesy Fehily Contemporary, Melbourne; Sean Miller: photo Anthony Stone; Tully Moore: courtesy John Buckley Gallery, Melbourne; Callum Morton: courtesy Anna Schwartz Gallery, Melbourne and Sydney; Arlo Mountford: courtesy Sutton Gallery, Melbourne; Elizabeth Newman: courtesy Neon Parc, Melbourne; photo Christian Capurro; Geoff Newton: courtesy Neon Parc, Melbourne; Tom Nicholson: courtesy Milani Gallery, Brisbane; photo the artist with Tristan da Roza Tomislav Nikolic: courtesy Jensen Gallery, Sydney; photo Andrew Jensen; John Nixon: courtesy Anna Schwartz Gallery, Melbourne and Sydney; Rose Nolan: courtesy Anna Schwartz Gallery, Melbourne and Sydney; photo John Brash; Simon Obarzanek: courtesy Karen Woodbury Gallery, Melbourne; Selina Ou: courtesy Sophie Gannon Gallery, Melbourne; Robert Owen: courtesy ARC ONE, Melbourne; Spiros Panigirakis: courtesy Sarah Scout, Melbourne; Polixeni Papapetrou: courtesy Nellie Castan Gallery, Melbourne, and Stills Gallery, Sydney; Perks and Mini / PAM: photo Max Doyle; Stieg Persson: courtesy Anna Schwartz

Gallery, Melbourne and Sydney; **Joshua Petherick:** Galerie Croy Nielsen, Berlin; photo Andrew Curtis; **Patricia Piccinini:** courtesy Tolarno Galleries, Melbourne; photo Peter Hennessey; **Patrick Pound:** courtesy Fehily Contemporary, Melbourne, Hamish McKay Gallery, Wellington, New Zealand, and Melanie Roger Gallery, Auckland, New Zealand; **Clare Rae:** courtesy Beam Contemporary, Melbourne; **Reko Rennie:** courtesy Karen Woodbury Gallery, Melbourne; **Stuart Ringholt:** courtesy Milani Gallery, Brisbane; **David Rosetzky:** courtesy Sutton Gallery, Melbourne; **Sangeeta Sandrasegar:** courtesy Murray White Room, Melbourne; photo John Brash; **Gareth Sansom:** Roslyn Oxley9 Gallery, Sydney, and Milani Gallery, Brisbane; **Yhonnie Scarce:** courtesy Dianne Tanzer Gallery and Projects, Melbourne; photo Janelle Low; **Nick Selenitsch:** courtesy Sutton Gallery, Melbourne; **Jan Senbergs:** courtesy Niagara Galleries, Melbourne; **Caleb Shea:** courtesy Utopian Slumps, Melbourne; **Slave Pianos:** courtesy Darren Knight Gallery, Sydney; photo Edwin 'Dolly' Roseno; **Glenn Sloggett:** courtesy Stills Gallery, Sydney; **Kate Smith:** courtesy Sutton Gallery, Melbourne; photo Andrew Curtis; **Charlie Sofo:** courtesy Darren Knight Gallery, Sydney; **Bryan Spier:** courtesy Sarah Scout, Melbourne; **Stelarc:** courtesy Scott Livesey Galleries, Melbourne; **Darren Sylvester:** courtesy Sullivan+Strumpf, Sydney; **David Thomas:** courtesy Nellie Castan Gallery, Melbourne, and Conny Dietzschold Gallery, Sydney; **Meredith Turnbull:** courtesy Pieces of Eight, Melbourne; **Peter Tyndall:** courtesy Anna Schwartz Gallery, Melbourne and Sydney; **Michelle Ussher:** courtesy KalimanRawlins, Melbourne, and Darren Knight Gallery, Sydney; **Ronnie van Hout:** courtesy KalimanRawlins Gallery, Melbourne; **Prue Venables:** courtesy Olsen Irwin Gallery, Sydney; photo Nick Hannah; **Daniel von Sturmer:** courtesy Anna Schwartz Gallery, Melbourne and Sydney; **David Wadelton:** courtesy Tolarno Galleries, Melbourne; **Jake Walker:** courtesy Utopian Slumps, Melbourne, and Gallery 9, Sydney; **Lisa Waup:** courtesy Baluk Arts, Mornington, Victoria; **Lydia Wegner:** courtesy ARC ONE, Melbourne; **Bradd Westmoreland:** courtesy Niagara Galleries, Melbourne; **Raymond Young:** photo Anthony Stone

First published in 2013 by
The Council of Trustees of
the National Gallery of Victoria
180 St Kilda Road
Melbourne, Victoria 3004, Australia
www.ngv.vic.gov.au

Published for the exhibition *Melbourne
Now*, NGV International, 180 St Kilda Road,
Melbourne, and The Ian Potter Centre:
NGV Australia, Federation Square,
22 November 2013 – 23 March 2014.

National Library of Australia Cataloguing-in-
Publication entry:

Title: Melbourne now exhibition guide /
        National Gallery of Victoria.
ISBN: 9780724103775 (pbk)
Subjects:
        Melbourne (Vic.)—Exhibitions.
        Melbourne (Vic.)—History—
        Exhibitions.
        Melbourne (Vic.)—Social life
        and customs—Exhibitions.
Other Authors/Contributors:
        National Gallery of Victoria, issuing
        body.
Dewey Number:
        994.51

Publications Manager: Jasmin Chua
Text editor: Mark Gomes
Senior Publications Coordinator:
    Jennie Moloney
Publications Coordinator: Megan Patty
Publications Assistant: Nadiah Abdulrahim
Proofreader: Eugenie Baulch
Designers: Thomas Deverall and
    Dirk Hiscock
Map illustrations: Connor Byrt
Pre-press: Rachael Brown, Justine Frost
    and Philip White
Printer: Adams Print
Cover stock: 300gsm Knight Linenboard
Text stock: 100gsm Pacesetter Laser Pro

This publication has been generously
supported by the Vizard Foundation.

Additional print support for this book has
been provided by Adams Print.

*Every effort has been made to contact
persons owning copyright in the works of art
illustrated in this publication. In cases where
this has not been possible owners are invited
to notify the Publications Department at
the National Gallery of Victoria. The views
expressed in this publication are those of the
authors and do not necessarily reflect those
of the NGV or the publisher.*

*This publication contains the names and
images of Indigenous people who have
passed away and which may cause distress
to some Indigenous people. Please note that
some records contain terms, annotations
and titles that reflect the period in which the
item was recorded, and may be considered
inappropriate today in some circumstances.
These are a reflection of past practices only
and do not reflect the current attitudes of the
National Gallery of Victoria, Melbourne.*

*Please note that indicative images of artists'
works have been included in this publication
in instances where the work for the exhibition
was not final at the time of printing.*

10 9 8 7 6 5 4 3 2

(cover)
Staircase Melbourne 2013
Photo: Dirk Hiscock